GPS –
GUIDING
PRINCIPLES FOR
SUCCESS

SCOTT GEORGE

GPS – GUIDING PRINCIPLES FOR SUCCESS

Copyright ©2016 by Scott George

ISBN: 978-1-939779-42-7

Published by

LifeBridge

BOOKS
P.O. BOX 49428
CHARLOTTE, NC 28277

CONTENTS

FOREWORD
BY U.S. CONGRESSMAN
DANIEL WEBSTER

Life is hard. Life is also good and sometimes unfair, but for the most part life is a beautiful gift given to us by our Creator.

I believe God gave us a book, specifically the Bible and the book of Proverbs, to serve as a guide and a tool to give us wisdom and insights in how to live our lives every day to honor Him. In great times of joy and happiness, as well as those of grief and sorrow, the words written in Proverbs help us navigate through uncharted waters with confidence and courage, knowing that we have One who can give us directions and warnings as we walk the steps of life.

For the past 32 years, I have read through the book of Proverbs each month. Very seldom does a day go by that I don't look to this inspiration to help me become a better person. I could not do what I do without the internal GPS that directs me in every decision I make. I am grateful and blessed because of the lessons I have learned from the book of Proverbs.

The wisest political leader of all time, Solomon, has

given us a great and valuable treasure. His words tell us how to stay safe in a very unsafe world.

I am honored to write the forward for this new and exciting book by Scott George: *GPS: Guiding Principles for Success.* These are timeless truths that will have a dynamic impact on your life.

I have known Scott for several years and have watched him live his life with the wisdom of Solomon by his dedicated service at the Community Food and Outreach Center in Downtown Orlando which helps hundreds of working poor families daily. Scott also serves the Pine Castle community at Pine Castle United Methodist Church faithfully and with passion.

I know what you are about to read will inspire and motivate you to stay on track and keep you living beyond the ordinary.

PREFACE
BY JIM GEORGE

When Scott George, our oldest son, asked me to write the Foreword for this book, I was shocked, yet honored.

In reflecting back on my 55-plus years as a pastor, I have found that plenty of people are smart, but only a few are wise. Solomon has the distinction of being the wisest man who ever lived.

In the 31 chapters of his book, he shares his wisdom on topics from temptations to relationships. Proverbs is a book that provides answers to our questions about everyday life. How sad that our society usually only offers opinions, yet answers are few and far between.

I spoke earlier of being shocked. When two pastors meet together for friendship and fellowship, generally the conversation will center on the question, "What are you preaching on? What are you teaching on?"

When Scott shared with me that he was speaking for one solid year on Proverbs, I was surprised. I have never heard of any minister focusing for over a year on just the book of Proverbs.

My first question was, "Why?" But the more I

thought about it, my response was, "Why not?"

So, buckle up, find a nice place to read and you will have an enjoyable experience learning from this marvelous book, *GPS – Guiding Principles for Success.*

– Pastor Jim George
Geneva United Methodist Church

DEDICATION

This book is dedicated to the faithful, loving members of Pine Castle United Methodist Church, Orlando, Florida, on its 110th anniversary.

The following is written by longtime member
Charlotte Louise Mott Yates

Dear Readers:

In God's book of Proverbs, our gracious, all-powerful, all-knowing, and all-loving Creator has shared with us His wisdom.

We find in these pages, pictures of how to live successfully, in contrast with statements of how to miss His pathway. He stands at every crossroad with clear signs to direct us to the way of really living, comparing it in pithy words to choosing a road that leads downward to utter chaos and confusion.

I have discovered that when I trust Him, honor others, and relate lovingly to my family of God, the results in me are peace and joy!

As I write this, I will be 96 years old on my next birthday. I have been young, and now I am old, and I have never seen the righteous forsaken or their seed begging bread.

I have found I can trust God absolutely; and He has found that He can rely on me to trust Him, no matter what.

I trust God with all my heart, and don't lean on my own understanding. In all my ways, I acknowledge Him and allow Him to direct my paths.

"Thank You, God, for being so gracious to Your creatures to give us such a treasure of Your wisdom that reveals to anyone who is truly seeking Your wise, narrow pathway. Through it, we discover the Way, the Truth, and the Life!"

In the pages of this book written by Pastor Scott, we will find the discernment that God's Holy Spirit has revealed to him for living a successful life. He is a man who has chosen the narrow road that leads upward. He has spent time focusing on God's face, listening to His wise words, then taking time to share with us what God has imparted to him! We will be blessed as we open our spirits, souls, and bodies to what God's Spirit has shown to Pastor Scott. We will be investing our time wisely as we trust God to put these revelations to work in our lives.

Our loving, heavenly Father is preparing each of us for eternity. There, we shall meet each other at the end of time, and have forever to rejoice together!

– Charlotte Louise Mott Yates

INTRODUCTION

There have been thousands of volumes written on success and personal achievement. However, there is one book that contains more wisdom than all the others combined—the Book of Proverbs.

It was written by Solomon, the son of King David, nearly a thousand years before Christ and zeros in on the one ingredient that is missing in the lives of most men and women: wisdom.

The topics found in Proverbs are amazing. They include:

- Adultery
- Anger
- Attitude
- Backsliding
- Business partnerships
- Character
- Child training
- Communication
- Conflict
- Courage
- Fear of the Lord
- Flattery

- Fools
- Forgiveness
- Friends
- Generosity
- Gossip
- Greed
- Guilt
- Happiness
- Love
- Marriage
- Mercy
- Money
- Obedience
- Parents
- Peer pressure
- Poverty
- Sexual relationships
- Sin
- Speech
- Stubbornness
- Thoughts
- Trouble
- Unity
- Vision
  — and the list goes on!

After preaching dozens of sermons based on Proverbs, I have focused on 12 specific "wisdom" themes from this marvelous book that will give you supernatural direction for your future.

Let me also encourage you to take the time to read Proverbs in its entirety. The 31 chapters are perfect for a month-long daily devotional.

To every issue, problem, or circumstance we encounter, God is saying, "I want you to be wise and live in safety, if you will only hear My words and put them into practice."

I pray that as a result of reading and applying the principles found on these pages you will become a better mom, dad, grandparent, student, business person, community leader—or whatever your role in life may be.

Long before the digital age, the Lord inspired Solomon to write the ultimate "global positioning system" that not only shows us where we are, but leads us on a wise, eternal path.

Get ready to receive and respond to God's *GPS—Guiding Principles for Success.*

– *Scott George*

1
WISDOM FOR LIFE

*The proverbs of Solomon son of David, king
of Israel: for gaining wisdom and instruction;
for understanding words of insight; for receiving
instruction in prudent behavior, doing what is right
and just and fair; for giving prudence to those who
are simple, knowledge and discretion to the young
—let the wise listen and add to their learning, and
let the discerning get guidance—for understanding
proverbs and parables, the sayings and riddles
of the wise. The fear of the Lord is the
beginning of knowledge, but fools
despise wisdom and instruction.*
– PROVERBS 1:1-7

I wish someone would have plopped me down 30
years ago and said, "Scott, I'm going to teach you the
book of Proverbs and what it means to be wise."

Thankfully, I took the initiative to delve into this
insightful book on my own, and I pray you will be able
to receive its truths and pass them onto your children

and to the generations to come.

Our time on earth can be complicated and we need God's wisdom to help us navigate through this journey called life. This is why we must be alert and aware, constantly asking our heavenly Father for His wisdom and GPS system for living. Jesus didn't sugar-coat the fact that *"In this world you will have trouble"* (John 16:33). Yes, at times things will be difficult, so as Christians and disciples we need to have divine input from above to steer us on the right path.

We can attempt to forge ahead under our own steam, skill, desire, or intellect, but that's only going to get us so far, But if you and I have the guidance that comes from God's Word and the principles He has given us, we will be able to stay on the Street called Success.

As a pastor, I constantly counsel with men and women who find themselves in devastating situations—heartbroken marriages, distressed children, and lives that come screeching to a halt. Why? Because godly wisdom was not applied and people make bad decisions. And we all know how one wrong choice can quickly mushroom into a full-blown tragedy.

You don't need to be the sharpest knife in the drawer, but it is vital to have the wisdom of God, which only comes by reading the Word and asking the Lord to fill you with His insight, and knowledge.

To become an individual who grows in wisdom, it only makes sense that we learn from the wise.

THE BILLION DOLLAR MAN

Proverbs was written primarily by a young man named Solomon, who became known as the wisest of all men.

In addition, he holds the title as one of the wealthiest individuals in recorded history. It has been calculated that by today's economic scale, Solomon was able to amass over $1 *billion* every year. Compound that over time and you have a glimpse of Solomon's earthly treasure.

The Bible tells us that Solomon *"spoke three thousand proverbs"* (1 Kings 4:32) which he could recite at any time—this is more than the 913 that he penned in the book of Proverbs.

Men and women from all over the world would make their way to his royal palace just to listen to this wise man. What an amazing legacy Solomon left by writing down these life-changing words through the unction and power of the Holy Spirit so you and I could avoid making wrong decisions and become wise.

As we begin, there are four question we need to ask:

Question #1: What is Wisdom?

Wisdom is the ability to navigate through life with good judgment.

I like that word navigate because life is a journey. You go to school, choose a career, get married, have children and grandkids. On more than one occasion I've heard people comment, "I wish there was a book that would help me prepare for life." Well, there is—and it's the Book of Proverbs.

It is estimated that the average adult makes over 35,000 decisions in one day—from responding to questions to changing lanes in traffic.

Pause for a moment and zero in on one circumstance you are currently facing that you need God's wisdom to help you plot a course through. Does it involve a personal relationship, a business decision, finances?

As you will discover, there is an answer to be found in Proverbs.

Question #2: Why do I need wisdom?

This gift from above is necessary because life is challenging and we need to know how to maneuver through its winding paths and detours.

In Sunday School, I heard the story dozens of times about the wise and foolish builders, and why we should construct our house on a solid foundation. As an adult, I now see how this truth applies to building on wisdom.

Jesus taught, *"Therefore everyone who hears these words of mine and puts them into practice is like a wise man who built his house on the rock. The rain came down, the streams rose, and the winds blew and beat against that house; yet it did not fall, because it had its foundation on the rock"* (Matthew 7:24-25).

The Lord is trying to bring each of us to that place where we are secure and don't crumble, crash, or burn. Why? Because a storm is brewing on the horizon, the waters will rise, and there will be tempests and torments. As Jesus cautioned, *"But everyone who hears these words of mine and does not put them into practice is like a foolish man who built his house on sand. The rain came down, the streams rose, and the winds blew and beat against that house, and it fell with a great crash"* (verses 26-27).

AN UNEXPECTED WARNING

A few years ago when I was a youth pastor, I was a guest speaker at a conference held at Oral Roberts University in Tulsa, Oklahoma. There were about 5,000 teenagers present from all over the country.

When you're a youth minister, you are supposed to be upbeat, energetic, and loads of fun!

There was an exciting atmosphere in the Mabee Center at ORU, but a few minutes before I was to address the crowd, God clearly spoke to my spirit, saying, "Scott George, the first words out of your mouth are to warn a youth pastor in the audience that he's getting ready to fall into adultery. I want you to tell him, because I need to grab his attention!"

Let me set the scene. As I was introduced, bright strobe lights were flashing, and a "smoke machine" was billowing. Internally, however, I was fighting a battle. "God, why? With all these kids in attendance, let me tell a joke or share something humorous." It was useless. The Lord had given me instructions and I knew there was no other option but to obey Him.

So when the applause died down, I looked out into the vast audience and without any hesitation, announced, "There is a youth pastor here and you are within minutes or hours of committing adultery. God has sent me to warn you that you must repent."

Talk about an eye-opener to a message! The kids' eyes were wide open. Some were nudging each other, wondering, "What's adultery?" They didn't have a clue what was going on, and I must admit that I was perplexed as to why the Lord had me make that statement at such a venue.

After finishing the message I had prepared, a man approached me, and he was weeping. Right there, he confessed that he was just a few hours away from making a tragic mistake, but because he listened to the rebuke of God, he was wise instead of foolish and allowed his spiritual house to stand firm on the Rock—Christ Jesus.

Question #3: Where does wisdom come from?

In the first chapter of Proverbs this question is clearly answered: *"The fear of the Lord is the beginning of knowledge, but fools despise wisdom and discipline"* (Proverbs 1:7).

So wisdom arrives when we develop a healthy respect and reverence for the Almighty.

Many display an arrogant attitude, believing they can do whatever they please—that life is good and they are mature enough to make their own decisions. Such a mindset leads us down a dead end street.

I'm so grateful for my grandma George. She was a Pentecostal, no-nonsense, black and white believer; a woman of prayer who stayed on a solid, spiritual track. She had a healthy fear of God and her influence—and the way she lived and walked—affected me.

Grandmas and grandpas: your children and grandchildren are constantly observing you. The most profound impact you can have on them is to live a life

21

that respects, honors, and stands in awe of the holy God. Never forget that the fear of the Lord is the beginning of wisdom and knowledge.

Solomon not only wrote Proverbs, but he was the author of Ecclesiastes. In his final chapter of that book, here is his summation, which I believe is the tipping point: *"Now all has been heard; here is the conclusion of the matter: Fear God and keep his commandments, for this is the whole duty of man. For God will bring every deed into judgment, including every hidden thing, whether it is good or evil"* (Ecclesiastes 12:13-14).

At one time or another, you've probably heard the KISS advice: "Keep It Simple, Stupid!" Well, Solomon boiled it down to this one principle: fear God and keep His commandments.

If we follow this directive, we will survive every circumstance.

Question #4: How do I obtain wisdom?

If you had a magic "genie in a bottle" and could make any wish that would come true, what would you ask for?

One person might dream, "I would like $100 million." Another may wish, "I'd like to become the most powerful person in the world." A third may say,

"I want to live in perfect health and never become sick."

Solomon didn't have a mythical genie, he had a relationship with a holy God who appeared to him one night and said, *"Ask for whatever you want me to give you"* (2 Chronicles 1:7). Wow! What an amazing offer!

Since Solomon was taking over the leadership of his father, King David, he requested only one thing: *"Lord God, let your promise to my father David be confirmed, for you have made me king over a people who are as numerous as the dust of the earth. Give me wisdom and knowledge, that I may lead this people, for who is able to govern this great people of yours?"* (verses 9-10).

Solomon knew that if he had divine insight, he could gain everything else.

God looked deep into the soul of Solomon and told him, *"Since this is your heart's desire and you have not asked for wealth, riches or honor, nor for the death of your enemies, and since you have not asked for a long life but for wisdom and knowledge to govern my people over whom I have made you king, therefore wisdom and knowledge will be given you. And I will also give you wealth, riches and honor, such as no king who was before you ever had and none after you will have"* (verses 11-12).

Many are walking through their hours and days

wishing and hoping for earthly gain, and the Lord promises they can be ours, but first we need to seek His wisdom.

God knows that some men and women are not capable of handling fortune or fame because their priorities are backwards; they fail to seek good judgement. Yes, He desires for you to be a successful businessperson, yet also to have wisdom in dealing with your employees. He wants you to enjoy a family, but have wisdom in knowing how to raise them.

How do you gain wisdom? Like Solomon, be bold and ask for it!

This was echoed by James in the New Testament: *"If any of you lacks wisdom, he should ask God, who gives generously to all without finding fault, and it will be given to you"* (James 1:5).

Your heavenly Father is omniscient—all knowing—and wants to give His insight to you today. Start asking!

ROYALTY AND FAVOR

Immediately after declaring, *"The fear of the Lord is the beginning of knowledge, but fools despise wisdom and discipline,"* Solomon wrote these words: *"Listen my son, to your father's instruction and do not forsake your mother's teaching. They will be a garland to grace your head and a chain to adorn your neck"* (Proverbs 1:8-9).

A garland is a symbol of royalty and a necklace speaks of God's blessing.

If the Lord allowed you to have godly parents who gave you instruction from the Word, be eternally thankful. If not, the Lord will make up for lost time. He says, "I am going to give you teachers, instructors, and people who will speak into your life." That's what church is all about—redeeming and replacing what the enemy has stolen.

When we walk in divine wisdom, we begin to live in a position of royalty. And when we hear and obey God's Word, we wear the necklace of our heavenly Father's favor.

You don't have to tell such a person that they are honored; this comes naturally with the territory and they walk in it. When we are wise in Christ the blessings follow automatically.

In this treasure trove called the book of Proverbs, Solomon is helping us build our lives, families, careers, and our church around something that's going to withstand the test of time. The key is opening our ears to hearing God's words and applying them.

THREE ESSENTIALS

Let me jump ahead to Proverbs 24 and you'll discover how to build a life that will last. Solomon writes, *"By wisdom a house is built, and through understanding it is established; and through knowledge its rooms are filled with rare and beautiful treasures"* (verse 3).

This verse contains three essential words:

1. Wisdom
2. Knowledge
3. Understanding

You will find them dozens of times in Solomon's writings. They are each unique.

Knowledge is information; and it answers the question, "What?" However, knowledge in and of itself is not going to get you where you need to be; success requires more.

I'm sure you've met individuals who are overflowing with information, but dumber than a bag of rocks! They're smart, have all the facts and data, can rattle off statistics and numbers, and they are brilliant. There's plenty to admire about them, yet there is a missing link.

Wisdom is the *application* of knowledge. It answers the question, "Why?"

Understanding is how all of this fits together; implementation. It answers the question "How?"

I call these "the three amigos." All three are necessary friends, and they work together to build a house that will endure the elements.

THE SEARCH

We must never forget that God is the author of wisdom, the author of knowledge, and the author of understanding. The good news is that when we seek Him, much more will be ours.

Solomon didn't pursue honor, wealth, power, or the destruction of his enemies. He humbly said, "God, I am seeking You. I want Your knowledge and understanding." That's when the floodgates of heaven burst wide open!

Jesus reminds us, *"Seek first the kingdom of God and his righteousness, and all these things shall be added to you"* (Matthew 6:33 NKJV).

What Solomon sought became a thread that runs

through both the Old and New Testaments. Paul the Apostle wrote, *"My purpose is that they may be encouraged in heart and united in love, so that they may have the full riches of complete **understanding**, in order that they may know the mystery of God, namely, Christ, in whom are hidden all the treasures of **wisdom** and **knowledge"** (Colossians 2:2-3).

The word "hidden" lets us know that we must seek and search for these priceless treasures—and be passionate in the process. They are all found in Christ, who will supply all we will ever need or dream of.

He holds the key to finding wisdom for life.

2

WISDOM FOR GUIDANCE AND PROTECTION

*My son, if you accept my words and store
up my commands within you, turning your
ear to wisdom and applying your heart to understanding—indeed, if you call out for insight and cry
aloud for understanding, and if you look for it as for
silver and search for it as for hidden treasure, then
you will understand the fear of the Lord and find
the knowledge of God. For the Lord gives wisdom;
from his mouth come knowledge and understanding. He holds success in store for the upright, he
is a shield to those whose walk is blameless,
for he guards the course of the just and
protects the way of his faithful ones.*

– PROVERBS 2:1-8

My wife, Tammi, and I have four children and
I'm a rather visual type person. So I try to illustrate to

our kids what it means to live in safety: I call it the "umbrella principle." I tell each of them, "Austen, Aaren, Allison, Amanda, if you want to be safe and wise, then listen to your mother and me when we offer instruction and advice. If you will listen to our words, you will live under a covering of safety. It's when you disobey and make choices outside of what we try to tell you to do as godly parents, that you step into the unknown, away from the umbrella, leaving the protection of God's security and wisdom."

The Lord desires for His children to live in safety; He wants us to grow to be men and women who are wise and obedient. If we decide to become rebellious, or confident in our own power, we will live beyond the covering of His divine umbrella and wind up getting drenched!

The very name, Solomon, means "to be safe." How appropriate. This wise man is tying to protect us from tragedy and disaster by teaching us how to walk in godly wisdom. At times he gets the point across by negative examples, showing us what will happen if we ignore the lessons of good judgement he shares.

FIVE MARVELOUS BENEFITS

In this second chapter of Proverbs, we discover five

benefits of heaven-sent wisdom:

Benefit #1: God's Wisdom Will Give You Victory

Solomon wrote: *"He holds victory in store for the upright..."* (Proverbs 2:7).

I once saw a TV commercial for Cadillac cars that showed a man licking an ice cream cone. The announcer enticingly said, "Vanilla. Some people can't get enough. But if you're in the mood for something tasty, then test drive the Cadillac SRX."

It reminded me of far too many who call themselves Christians, but they're also just plain vanilla —ho-hum and bland. But that's not the life God intends for us to live. There are plenty of delightful options awaiting us.

When I watch the finals of the National Basketball Association, I never see players who wake up that morning thinking, "Oh, man, I can't wait to get slam dunked today!" Instead they hit the floor with enthusiasm and the expectation that they are going to be champions.

When you apply the Word to your walk, you can be assured that even though you may make a few mistakes along the way, you can say, "I am victorious through Christ."

31

Benefit #2: God's Wisdom Will Shield You From Your Enemies

The second half of Proverbs 2:7 tells us, *"...he is a shield to those whose walk is blameless."*

The Almighty is your armor and protective covering and He is prepared to fight your battles for you. As you increase in wisdom, knowledge, and understanding, He becomes a strong defense against your foes.

Benefit #3: God's Wisdom Will Guard You and Keep You on the Right Path

We have this awesome guarantee: *"For he guards the course of the just and protects the way of his faithful ones"* (Proverbs 2:8).

I don't know about you, but there have been times when the GPS on my phone had a digital hiccup and I found myself way off course. I had five minutes to reach my destination, but I was lost—and almost lost my religion!

Life is too short to veer off track. Looking at the broader picture, if you are "off" just one percent each week, by the end of the year, you're miles away from your intended target. When this happens you find yourself out in the woods, trying to find your bearings, wasting precious time and energy,

This is why we need to continually pray, "Lord,

give me Your wisdom—Your Guiding Principles for Success—that will keep me on the right path.

Benefit #4: God's Wisdom Will Protect You From Harm

Here is another promise: *"Discretion will protect you, and understanding will guard you."* (Proverbs 2:11).

One beautiful morning last spring, I saw an ad on television that really put a guilt trip on me. Home Depot was telling me that it was time to plant some flowers.

Their investment in advertising worked! I drove to the store and bought a few flats and spent the whole afternoon planting a rainbow of colors in my front yard. Before sunset, tired but happy, I stood back and admired my handiwork.

However, the next morning, when I looked out-side, I could hardly believe my eyes. A squirrel had burrowed into my flowers, and to add insult to injury, had eaten half of them!

I was so upset that I wanted to get a shotgun and find that squirrel, but I knew my neighbors wouldn't approve. So I came up with a better idea.

I went to a garden store and bought two big 14" fake owls, secured them on poles, and stuck them in the flower beds.

Success. It worked!

Life, however, is so much more than having a picture-perfect front yard. When you walk in God's wisdom, understanding, and knowledge, you can relax and have confidence that you are protected from harm, and that the one who is shielding you is not a $15 imitation owl, but Almighty God.

Benefit #5: God's Wisdom Will Save You From Wicked Influences

How good to know that *"Wisdom will save you from the ways of wicked men, from men whose words are perverse"* (Proverbs 2:12).

Those in the business world are well aware of how an autocratic boss with the wrong motives can make life miserable. It's just one reason why we need to tap into godly insight that can give us the bigger picture —and save us from yielding to the wrong influences.

GET IN THE "ZONE"

Throughout the book of Proverbs, the Lord is telling us that He has our back if we will simply seek after His ways. In the very first chapter we are told, *"...whoever listens to me will live in safety and be at ease, without fear of harm"* (Proverbs 1:33).

A major objective should be to stay in the zone of loving and seeking God, then allow these forces to protect, guard, and lead us. This is where we find shelter, peace, and contentment.

We have choices: we can either live exposed to the elements of this world, or we can get into the flow where God is protecting us—where we discover satisfaction and joy.

Have you ever watched the Daytona 500 or a major NASCAR race? I'm not a physics major or a race car driver, but I have learned that the person who usually wins is the individual who stays behind the lead car for most of the race. You see, the car in front, going 200 miles an hour, is taking the full force of the wind. So the smart driver will draft behind him, almost to the last lap, then swing out and boost forward to capture the checkered flag.

As a believer, draft behind God's momentum of wisdom, knowledge, and understanding. When you do, the hard work is done—and you are headed for victory.

Sadly, so many are not staying close enough to the Lord's leading. On the race course of life we think we have all the answers and brag, "God, I've got this covered. I'm going to stay in another lane for a little while and meander over here for a few moments."

What the Lord provided is plowing forward while

we are chasing rabbits. Guess what happens? We find ourselves in the wrong zone and are exposed to the enemy, and before long the influences of the world begin to both attract and attack us. We then become vulnerable and unprotected because we are not drafting behind the Spirit of God.

SUPERNATURAL SAFETY

Those who *"walk in the ways of good men and keep to the paths of the righteous...will live in the land, and the blameless will remain in it; but the wicked will be cut off from the land, and the unfaithful will be torn from it"* (Proverbs 2:20-22).

The benefits of staying on the right course are enormous, but there's a terrible price to pay when we say, "I'll do it my way!"

How much better to live under the supernatural forces of God's safe keeping.

As the psalmist wrote, *"Blessed is the man who does not walk in the counsel of the wicked or stand in the way of sinners or sit in the seat of mockers. But his delight is in the law of the Lord, and on his law he meditates day and night. He is like a tree planted by streams of water, which yields its fruit in season and whose leaf does not wither. Whatever he does prospers"* (Psalm 1:1-3).

We not only have the blessing of protection, but the bonus of wisdom and prosperity!

Ultimate Victory

The man or woman who lives in true abundance, is the one who understands the ways and the words of God. He is diligently seeking the three *friends*—wisdom, knowledge, and understanding. This results in ultimate victory.

At the Olympic games, practically every athlete who stands on a podium proudly representing their country to receive a bronze, silver, or gold medal, has tears streaming down their cheeks. But they are tears of joy and celebration—being overcome by the thrill of victory.

In that instant, all the years of practice, pain, and perseverance are suddenly a reality. It is a special moment they will replay in their minds for as long as they draw breath.

Today, you have something to celebrate too. Because you have chosen to seek wisdom, the Lord has become your shield. He truly *"guards the course of the just and protects the way of his faithful ones"* (Proverbs 2:8).

So rejoice!

3

WISDOM FOR HUMILITY

*Trust in the Lord with all your heart
and lean not on your own understanding;
in all your ways submit to him, and he will
make your paths straight. Do not be wise in
your own eyes; fear the Lord and shun
evil. This will bring health to your body
and nourishment to your bones.*
– PROVERBS 3:5-8

I'm sure you've been around people who walk into a room with an attitude of, "Pay attention! I've arrived!" They don't have to utter a word, but you can sense, almost taste, their spirit of superiority.

It's the man or woman with this aura of arrogance that Solomon is addressing when he writes, *"Do not be wise in your own eyes."*

Countless millions have memorized the opening words of Proverbs 3, that if we trust in the Lord rather than leaning on our own understanding, He will make our crooked paths straight. However, they seem to ignore the next verse that warns us against becoming wise in our own eyes.

I am totally convinced that if we truly walk a life of humility, it will give us the power to accomplish the first objective—of trusting in the Lord.

Without question, your Creator desires for you to be wise, but not in your own estimation.

Pride has been defined as "an undue sense of one's superiority." Its focus is conceit or excessive self-esteem.

When I began to reflect on these words found in Proverbs, I was reminded of the story of a young man who had the hand of God resting on his life and was extremely successful. But that was before pride stepped into the picture!

It's the account of Uzziah—one of the descendants of Solomon (see Matthew 1:7-8).

Scripture records, *"Uzziah was sixteen years old when he became king, and he reigned in Jerusalem fifty-two years. His mother's name was Jecoliah; she was from Jerusalem. He did what was right in the eyes of the Lord, just as his father Amaziah had done. He sought God during the days of Zechariah, who instructed him in the fear of God. As long as he sought the Lord, God gave him success"* (2 Chronicles 26:3-5).

Seeking the Lord was part of Uzziah's legacy. His

father's name, Amaziah, means "God is mighty," and his mother's name, Jecoliah, stands for "God is able."

His parents instructed their son daily: "Uzziah, I want you to understand that God is strong, powerful, and able to do the impossible." They named their son Uzziah, which means, "God is my strength."

It should not be surprising to see what this man accomplished, even at the young age of sixteen. Every morning he would arise saying, "God, I have been taught that You are mighty, You are able, and You are making me strong."

As a result, whatever project he tackled was blessed by the Great Jehovah. As Scripture tells us, *"As long as he sought the Lord, God gave him success"* (verse 5).

When you read the next few verses you will discover Uzziah's accomplishments. The word "he" and "his" are used 16 times, including:

- *"He...broke down the walls of Gath, Jabneh and Ashdod"* (verse 6).
- *"He...rebuilt towns near Ashdod"* (verse 6).
- *"...his fame spread as far as the border of Egypt, because he had become very powerful"* (verse 8).
- *"He also built towers in the wilderness and dug many cisterns, because he had much livestock in the foothills and in the plain"* (verse 10).

- *"He had people working his fields and vineyards in the hills and in the fertile lands"* (verse 10).
- *"[He] had a well-trained army"* (verse 11).
- *"His fame spread far and wide"* (verse 15).

I wasn't there, but I get the impression that Uzziah started to see his name emblazoned everywhere and developed the "big head." Instead of reaping success *"because he sought the Lord"* (verse 5), he was now waking up thinking how smart and capable he was.

What was the result? *"But after Uzziah became powerful, his pride led to his downfall. He was unfaithful to the Lord his God, and entered the temple of the Lord to burn incense on the altar of incense"* (verse 16).

His self-importance became so dominant that he walked into the Temple and thought he could do whatever he wanted. God had established a clear line of demarcation between the roles of kings and priest, but Uzziah didn't care. He decided to burn incense on the Temple's altar—which was strictly forbidden.

I can see the chief priest begging the king, "Please, no! Uzziah, you can't do this! Don't you understand that your father trained you to know that God was mighty? Your mother taught you to believe that God was able. Uzziah, I want to remind you that your name means 'God is my strength.' I am warning you, please don't do this!"

Uzziah didn't listen, even after being told, *"Leave the sanctuary, for you have been unfaithful; and you will not be honored by the Lord God"* (verse 18).

The king's self-centered, haughty disobedience lead to a disastrous result. Scripture tells us, *"Uzziah, who had a censer in his hand ready to burn incense, became angry. While he was raging at the priests in their presence before the incense altar in the Lord's temple, leprosy broke out on his forehead"* (verse 19).

If you think God isn't serious when He tells you that conceit leads to a catastrophe, think again!

FIVE WARNING SIGNS OF PRIDE

How can you know that you are on a downward slippery slope from first saying "God is my strength" to "I am wise in my own eyes"?

Instead of reading your own press clippings, here are a few red flags regarding runaway pride:

Warning Sign #1: An Excessive Drive to Maintain Outward Appearance While Neglecting Inward Character

Beware when you find yourself focusing on image,

marketing, and P.R. These are clues that you've decided that your worth is calculated by the exterior instead of what is on the inside.

When Uzziah became more concerned with his outward appearance than his inward character, he was headed for disaster.

Warning Sign #2: Struggling in Submitting to Godly Authority

Without question, the person who resists those who are either legally or spiritually in charge, has an ego problem.

The question becomes: who has godly authority? I believe it includes anyone who is placed in a role of leadership—from a member of the local police force to the usher who leads you to a seat in church.

If your first reaction is to balk at the order which has been established, you are having an issue with pride.

Listen to Uzziah who is crying out to you: "It happened to me. I walked through this first hand. I went from being successful to becoming a leper in a matter of years because I did not accept and react properly to godly authority."

Mom, the way you treat your child's kindergarten teacher sets an example. For instance, your kid comes home with a negative note in their backpack from the teacher or principle, and you immediately fly off the handle, not knowing all the details.

Is it any wonder your child takes on a bad attitude and is having a tough time in school? Could he or she have learned it from you?

Be careful how you respond to those God has placed over us—from governmental leaders to Sunday School teachers. As Christians, we must receive God-given authority properly.

Warning Sign #3: An Over-Estimation of One's Abilities and Accomplishments

It's human nature to be proud of driving a fancy car, living in an opulent home, and bragging about the size of your 401K, but those things can disappear in an unexpected moment.

According to Scripture, *"You may say to yourself, 'My power and the strength of my hands have produced this wealth for me.' But remember the Lord your God, for it is he who gives you the ability to produce wealth"* (Deuteronomy 8:17-18).

Uzziah over-estimated his personal achievements. He woke up one day, puffed with pride, boasting, "Look what I've accomplished." Then God said, "Oh yeah? We'll see."

It was quite a fall from luxury to leprosy!

Warning Sign #4: An Arrogant Perception that the World Centers Around You

It comes as a big shock to some people when their boss hands them a pink slip. They've been operating under the myth that no one could ever replace them.

They personify what the prophet Isaiah wrote about long ago: *"Your wisdom and knowledge mislead you when you say to yourself, 'I am, and there is none besides me'"* (Isaiah 47:10).

I've met a few individuals who could have had those last eight words printed on their t-shirt!

May I let you in on a little secret? The world doesn't revolve around you—or me. Relax and realize that there are many points of view and the opinions of others have merit and value.

As a pastor, I have to inwardly chuckle at times when I hear people grumble, "The sanctuary's too cold," "The music's too loud," or "We need more preaching about..."— etc., etc.

I realize that it's impossible to have a church that is centered around the opinions or perceptions of one person. Long ago I came to the conclusion that if just one life is changed in a service, it's worth all the time and effort. There will be occasions when the message or the music doesn't apply to our situation, but we should be in prayer for those who desperately need what is presented.

Warning Sign #5: Thriving on Public Recognition and Praise

If you want to root out pride, try hanging out with the homeless.

You might find this hard to believe, but there are sales clerks at Macy's or Target who may be living in their cars—trying to save enough money for the first month's deposit on an apartment.

As co-founder of the Community Food and Outreach Center in Orlando, I can tell you tragic stories of people who are destitute. One of the biggest misconceptions is that the ranks of the poor are filled with those who are mentally ill, disabled, or stay-at-home moms with too many kids. Far from it. Roughly half of those in need are the working poor. They are part of the labor force, but find it impossible to make ends meet.

Sure, we'd rather rub elbows with those who seem to have it all together, but let me invite you to spend time with the underprivileged and those who are struggling. It will keep your life in balance. Paul the Apostle nailed it when he wrote, *"Live in harmony with one another; do not be haughty, but associate with the lowly; never be conceited"* (Romans 12:16).

If you are consumed with your own self-image and importance, people will forget about the battles you won, the accomplishments you achieved, and the towers you built. When you are no longer concerned about God's strength, but are trying to look good in your own eyes, like Uzziah, your legacy will forever be tarnished.

When his life was over, the Bible tells us, *"Uzziah rested with his fathers and was buried near them in a field for burial that belonged to the kings, for people said, 'He had leprosy'"* (2 Chronicles 26:23).

This is a sobering reminder to all of us.

WHAT'S IT ALL ABOUT?

This is not the first time we have seen such a story play out. Think for a moment of some of our church leaders and politicians who started on the right path, trusting in the strength that only the Lord can supply. Suddenly they have a few successes under their belt and it soon becomes, "All about me!"—and nothing about God.

I pray these word will cause you to recommit your life to the principles you learned from your mother, father, and from God's Word. May you honestly be able to declare:

- "I am trusting in the Lord with all my heart."
- "I am not leaning on my own understanding."
- "In all my ways I am submitting to You, Lord."
- "I am asking You to make my paths straight."

- "I will not be wise in my own eyes."
- "I will fear the Lord and shun evil."

What is the result of such a commitment? *"This will bring health to your body and nourishment to your bones"* (Proverbs 3:8).

Humility is part of God's prescription for wisdom.

4

WISDOM FOR TEMPTATION

My son, keep my words and store up my commands within you. Keep my commands and you will live; guard my teachings as the apple of your eye. Bind them on your fingers; write them on the tablet of your heart. Say to wisdom, "You are my sister," and to insight, "You are my relative." They will keep you from the adulterous woman, from the wayward woman with her seductive words.

– PROVERBS 7:1-5

All of us, at any given time, can be guilty of committing adultery. It is not always sexual. Jesus said to the church at Ephesus, *"I have this against you, that you have left your first love"* (Revelation 2:4).

You can abandon your first love over money, alcohol, or habits, to name just a few enticements. You can commit adultery against God with pride, food, hobbies, etc. We need to be constantly reminded that the number one object of our affection must be Christ Jesus.

Although this chapter deals specifically with sexual infidelity, any of us are capable of giving our heart to something or someone else.

Repeatedly, Solomon warns us against the spirit of adultery that has ruined millions of marriages over the years—and through his counsel he is trying to keep us safe. His words are a stark reminder that we must be watchful and aware, never thinking we are above temptation, regardless of our age.

The Florida Department of Health recently released a statement saying: "Central Florida, where The Villages and other retirement communities sprawl across several counties, reported that cases of syphilis and chlamydia increased 71 percent among those 55 and older...and South Florida saw a 60 percent rise in those two sexually transmitted infections among the same age group."

So it doesn't matter what season of life you are in, it is imperative to pay attention when God's Word challenges you to stay pure in an immoral generation.

It's appalling how the media portrays adultery as something glamorous, even "normal." At times I want to yell out to the television set, "That's a bunch of crock!"

Please understand. If you have fallen into adultery

and you're living with remorse and guilt, I am not writing this to condemn you or deepen the pain. Hopefully, you've asked for God's forgiveness and you are moving forward.

If you have never fallen into this trap, I pray these words will inspire you to remain pure, righteous, and holy, and to honor the vow you made to your husband or wife, "forsaking all others" as long as you both shall live.

THREE CATEGORIES OF ADULTERY

The Bible has much to say concerning temptation —which always precedes infidelity. The arrows Satan uses in his devious arsenal include allurement, enticement, and finally seduction. They are used to break down our will power and make it easier for us to submit to his evil plans.

In Scripture, we find three categories of adultery:

Category #1: The Wayward Christian
In the first chapter of James we read: *"When tempted, no one should say, 'God is tempting me.' For God cannot be tempted by evil, nor does he tempt anyone; but each one is tempted when, by his own evil desire..."* (James 1:13-14).

The word *desire* is translated as "lust." Notice that we can't blame the devil for this; we are being dragged down by our own personal lust.

Far too often we blame Satan for things he's not really involved in. When you or I are tempted, it comes from within; it is our own evil desire and emotion that is being stirred.

James continues that after a person is ensnared by his personal wicked cravings, *"...he is dragged away and enticed. Then, after desire has conceived, it gives birth to sin; and sin, when it is full-grown, gives birth to death"* (verses 14-15).

Look at the six levels of progression:

1. *"dragged away"*
2. *"enticed"*
3. *"conceived"*
4. *"sin"*
5. *"birth"*
6. *"death"*

Whether we are talking about a member of the opposite sex (or in some cases the *same* sex), alcoholic beverages, or your thirst for power, it originates with a feeling called "lust." If it is not contained, controlled, or disciplined, you are eventually pulled in the wrong direction. It may take a minute, a day, or a week, but that evil force within you is suddenly activated and you are being dragged away.

Again, you are not being kidnaped by the devil, but by the perverse craving that is lurking deep inside. Sure, that is Satan's objective, but you make it so easy for him!

After progressing from being dragged away to being enticed, we are almost halfway through the process. At that stage we may foolishly think, "I've got this under control. Everything's going to be fine." But before we know it, our desire has conceived and given birth to sin and eventual death!

This is why James writes: *"Don't be deceived, my dear brothers"* (James 1:16).

What starts with a mere thought can quickly turn to unbridled passion, and eventual destruction.

Category #2: The Wayward Adulterer

If you want to avoid this entrapment, don't shirk your responsibilities. This was a lesson King David learned the hard way:

> *In the spring, at the time when kings go off to war, David sent Joab out with the king's men and the whole Israelite army. They destroyed the Ammonites and besieged Rabbah. But*

David remained in Jerusalem.

One evening David got up from his bed and walked around on the roof of the palace. From the roof he saw a woman bathing. The woman was very beautiful, and David sent someone to find out about her. The man said, "Isn't this Bathsheba, the daughter of Eliam and the wife of Uriah the Hittite?"

Then David sent messengers to get her. She came to him, and he slept with her. (She had purified herself from her uncleanness.) Then she went back home. The woman conceived and sent word to David, saying, "I am pregnant" (2 Samuel 11:1-5).

David was supposed to be with his armies on the front lines of the battlefield, but he remained in Jerusalem. When you're in the wrong place at the wrong time, you are giving opportunity for your impulsive desires and opening the door for the enemy to seize the moment.

King David probably rationalized, "I've worked hard, I'm successful, things are going well, so I will send the troops into battle and chill out here in Jerusalem for awhile. There, relaxing on his rooftop, he looked over the horizon and saw a woman bathing.

At the time, he didn't know her name was

Bathsheba—which means "daughter of promise." If he had, perhaps he would not have followed through with his lust.

This "daughter of promise" didn't ask for this encounter. She was minding her own business, leisurely enjoying a bath.

The actions David took directly parallel the six levels of progression we discussed regarding James 1:14-15:

1. *"The woman was very beautiful"* (2 Samuel 11:2). Seeing this naked female stirred his evil desires to be pulled, or "dragged away."
2. *"Then David sent messengers to get her. She came to him..."* (verse 4). She was "enticed."
3. The Bible says, *"...and he slept with her...Then the woman conceived and sent word to David, "I am pregnant"* (verses 4-5)." She "conceived."
4. To cover his transgression, David conspired to have Bathsheba's husband, Uriah, killed in battle (verses 6-24). That is "sin."
5. Bathsheba became David's wife *"and bore him a son"* (verse 27). The "birth."
6. David confessed his sin, but Nathan the prophet told him, *"...the son born to you will die"* (2 Samuel 12:14). Seven days later, that

is exactly what happened (verse 18). That is "death."

This is the reality of what takes place when we fail to follow God's orders. We need to be reminded that adultery is painful; it destroys marriages and ministries. It turns daughters of promise into victims and brings godly leaders to the point of death.

I can't count the number of men and women I have counseled who have faced the grief and sorrow of adultery. It leaves permanent scars on wives, husbands, and children. In the case of pastors, it impacts an entire congregation. The waves ripple through the community which now views that minister, church leader, or politician with scorn and shame.

It's not like a 30 minute television episode that quickly fades to black. It takes years of restoration to heal the wounds of infidelity. It's destructive, painful, and death-producing. Do not be fooled or deceived by your emotions!

PAYING FOR THE LAMB

After Bathsheba bore David a son, the Lord sent the prophet Nathan to David. The man of God told him this story:

> *There were two men in a certain town, one rich and the other poor. The rich man had a very large number of sheep and cattle, but the poor man had nothing except one little ewe lamb he had bought. He raised it, and it grew up with him and his children. It shared his food, drank from his cup and even slept in his arms. It was like a daughter to him.*
>
> *Now a traveler came to the rich man, but the rich man refrained from taking one of his own sheep or cattle to prepare a meal for the traveler who had come to him. Instead, he took the ewe lamb that belonged to the poor man and prepared it for the one who had come to him* (2 Samuel 12:1-4).

King David, not realizing that Nathan was referring to him, "*burned with anger against the man and said to Nathan, 'As surely as the Lord lives, the man who did this deserves to die! He must pay for that lamb four times over, because he did such a thing and had no pity.' Then Nathan said to David, 'You are the man!'*" (verses 5-7).

The phrase to circle is, "He must pay for that lamb four times." And David certainly did:

- First, the baby he had with Bathsheba died (2 Samuel 12:19).
- Second, David's son, Amnon, raped his half-sister, Tamar (2 Samuel 13:14).
- Third, Tamar's full brother, Absalom, killed Amnon for raping his sister (2 Samuel 13:22,28-29).
- Fourth, Absalom started a civil war to overthrow David and take over the kingdom, and Absalom died in battle (2 Samuel 18:15).

David paid the price for his adulterous act—not once, not twice, but four times. This is what happens when we let down our guard and succumb to carnal desires.

Category #3: The Wayward Adulteress

In Proverbs 7, Solomon describes how at sunset he looked out of the window of his house and saw a young man walking down the street. What took place next paints a sordid picture of seduction:

> Then out came a woman to meet him, dressed like a prostitute and with crafty intent. (She is unruly and defiant, her feet never stay at home; now in the street, now in the squares, at every

corner she lurks.)

She took hold of him and kissed him and with a brazen face she said: "Today I fulfilled my vows, and I have food from my fellowship offering at home. So I came out to meet you; I looked for you and have found you!"

"I have covered my bed with colored linens from Egypt. I have perfumed my bed with myrrh, aloes and cinnamon. Come, let's drink deeply of love till morning; let's enjoy ourselves with love! My husband is not at home; he has gone on a long journey. He took his purse filled with money and will not be home till full moon."

With persuasive words she led him astray; she seduced him with her smooth talk. All at once he followed her like an ox going to the slaughter, like a deer stepping into a noose till an arrow pierces his liver, like a bird darting into a snare, little knowing it will cost him his life. (Proverbs 7:10-23).

This is the same pattern of enticement that leads to destruction. It is why Solomon warns, *"Now then, my sons, listen to me; pay attention to what I say. Do not let your heart turn to her ways or stray into her paths. Many are the victims she has brought down; her slain are a mighty throng. Her house is a highway to the grave, leading down to the chambers of death"* (verses 24-27).

The Wayward Christian, the Wayward Adulterer, and the Wayward Adulterous; they all walk this very treacherous path. You are naïve if you think that just because you are a believer, a godly business person, or a single mom that you are above such temptation. As the gospel writer James tells us, "Don't be deceived" —you are not immune; it can happen to you.

I recently came across a list of "Consequences of Adultery" written by Jay Philip when he was a student at Phoenix Seminary. It includes:

- My relationship with God would suffer from a break in fellowship.
- I would suffer the emotional consequences of guilt.
- I would spend countless hours replaying the failure.
- My spouse would suffer the scars of this abuse more deeply than I could ever describe.
- My spouse would spend countless hours in counseling.
- My spouse's recovery would be long and painful.

- My spouse's pain would grieve me deeply and impound my own suffering and shame.
- Our relationship would suffer a break in trust, fellowship and intimacy.
- The reputation of my family would suffer loss.
- My sons, my daughters, would be deeply disappointed and bewildered.
- My grandchildren would not understand.
- My friends would be disappointed and would question my integrity.
- My witness among my neighbors would become worthless.
- My witness to my family would become shameful.
- My testimony among my spouse's family would be damaged.
- I would suffer God's discipline.
- Satan would be thrilled at my failure.
- Satan would work overtime to be sure that my shame never departed.
- My spouse might divorce me.
- My children might never speak to me.
- Our mutual friends would shy away from us and break fellowship.
- I would bring emotional pain to the woman, or man.
- I would bring reproach upon that other person.

- If that other person is married, their spouse might attempt to harm me.
- An unwanted child could be produced.
- My part in conception might trigger an abortion, the killing of an innocent child.
- Disease might result.
- Some might conclude that all Christians are hypocrites.
- My business, or occupation, may fail because I couldn't be trusted
- My leadership among those I have led in the past might also be diminished in impact.

Before you jump into this death chamber with another man or another woman, perhaps you should read this list once more. Maybe, just maybe, this might prevent you from living in deception.

I don't apologize for giving you a somber warning and charge. If this saves one marriage, if it salvages one relationship, it it all worthwhile.

With deep humility, we need to recognize that if moral failure can happen to David—a man after God's own heart (Acts 13:22)—it can happen to anyone.

5

WISDOM FOR LIFE'S STORMS

When the storm has swept by, the wicked
are gone, but the righteous stand firm forever.
— PROVERBS 10:25

It was the spring of 1986. My wife, Tammi, and I
had just moved from Orlando, Florida, to Oklahoma
City, where I had accepted a position as a youth
pastor. It was an exciting time for us as we had
purchased our first home in the suburb of Edmond.

We had heard that Edmond was situated in what is
called "Tornado Alley," but all of us were somewhat
innocent as to the ferocity of such storms.

After we'd been there a couple of months and
settled in, Tammi's sister, who was a cheerleader at
Florida State, came for a visit.

As we were preparing dinner one evening, an
emergency bulletin flashed on the television screen
and the announcer said with great urgency, "There is
a tornado headed for Edmond, Oklahoma. If you are

in Edmond, take cover now!"

As I rushed out the back door to turn off the barbecue grill, I looked south and lo and behold there was a huge tornado barreling straight for our neighborhood.

Not knowing what to expect, we all huddled in the pantry.

That Thursday, May 8, 1986, at 6:12 PM, we heard what sounded like a freight train headed straight for us. Thank God, we were spared, but when we were able to walk outside, it was one of the most devastating sights I'd ever seen. This F3 category tornado, with winds of up to 200 mph, cut a swath through our neighborhood that leveled dozens of homes, filling hospitals with the injured.

Later, as I had time to reflect on that frightening experience I realized that, even though materially we didn't own much, what we had could have been gone in a matter of seconds—including us! It was a life lesson I will never, ever forget.

NOT IF, BUT WHEN!

The storms each of us face on life's journey are not always accompanied by howling winds, waves, or hail, most of them are spiritual and emotional, impacting our hearts, souls, and minds.

Let's face facts. You and I are either in a storm, recovering from one, or getting ready to go through one. It's not a matter of *if,* but *when!*

This is why Solomon said: *"When the storm has swept by...* (Proverbs 10: 25). Who will be left standing firm? *"...the righteous."*

One of the most dramatic accounts in Scripture is that of a man who faced overwhelming obstacles. It is found in Acts 27—when Paul the Apostle was arrested in Jerusalem, bound in chains, and placed on a ship with other prisoners headed for Rome.

Four Storm-Surviving Principles

On the voyage to Italy, a dangerous storm erupted that threatened the lives of everyone on board. Paul's description of what took place contains four powerful lessons that will help us weather the squalls of life.

Principle #1: Storms Arrive Suddenly and Happen to Everyone

At sea, Paul, a man of God, issued this prophetic warning, *"'Men, I can see that our voyage is going to be disastrous and bring great loss to ship and cargo, and to our own lives also.' But the centurion, instead of listening to what Paul said, followed the advice of the pilot and of the owner of the ship"* (Acts 27:10-11).

After stocking up on supplies at a small port, Paul writes, *"When a gentle south wind began to blow... they weighed anchor and sailed along the shore of Crete. Before very long, a wind of hurricane force, called the Northeaster, swept down from the island. The ship was caught by the storm and could not head into the wind; so we gave way to it and were driven along"* (verses 13-15).

Principle #2: There is No Guarantee That You Will Have Warning When a Storm Crops Up

In Edmond, Oklahoma, we were fortunate to have a television announcer give us an advance warning: "Take cover!" But for the tempests that are bearing down on our inner man, we don't have the luxury of an email that says, "Today a storm is going to hit your life." Nor do we have a personal meteorologist to predict the day, the time, or the hour.

As believers, we need to be constantly ready so that when the gathering clouds are dark and ominous, we can look up and declare, *"My help comes from the Lord, the Maker of heaven and earth"* (Psalm 121:1).

Principle #3: Storms Give You the Opportunity to Evaluate What is Really Important

Paul, his fellow prisoners, and the captain of the ship, thought they had adequate supplies to make it to Rome, but in the midst of the turmoil, they knew it was time to lighten the load. The apostle writes, *"We took such a violent battering from the storm that the next day they began to throw the cargo overboard"* (Acts 27:18).

When you and I are faced with raging winds and rough waves, it gives us the opportunity to assess what is truly of value—and what can be discarded. There will come a time when you must make the decision, "What will I hold onto? What will I let go?"

In your hour of testing, God may be urging you to release what is *good* so you will cling to what is *great!* There may be things you've been holding onto for years that have helped you in previous storms, but that's no guarantee they will do the same through this crisis.

Perhaps today is the time to take a personal inventory and decide what you need to release in order to save your life and set you free. It could be a hobby, certain friends, or some activity that is absorbing all your time.

Don't depend on someone else to do the

evaluation, it must be between you and God.

Principle #4: Storms Reveal Your Hopelessness and Require Courage

In the natural, there are times when you may wonder if the skies will ever clear. Paul felt exactly the same way because he wrote, *"When neither sun nor stars appeared for many days and the storm continued raging, we finally gave up all hope of being saved"* (verse 20).

In each one of us, at different levels, distress and difficulties trigger fear, anxiety, and often hopelessness swells to the surface.

But allow me to share the good news! Storms have the potential to bring out one of the greatest character qualities you will ever possess—courage!

As the tempest raged in the Mediterranean Sea and those on board had gone many days without food, Paul stood before his fellow prisoners and their captors, saying, *"Men, you should have taken my advice not to sail from Crete; then you would have spared yourselves this damage and loss. But now I urge you to keep up your courage, because not one of you will be lost; only the ship will be destroyed"* (verses 21-22).

You may doubt your vessel is seaworthy enough to

withstand the turbulent winds and the tsunami-like waves. The enemy will whisper in your ear:

- "This is going to consume you."
- "You're going to go bankrupt."
- "You're going to lose your house."
- "You're going to lose your marriage."
- "You're not going to make it."
- "You're going to die."

Refuse to listen to Satan's menacing threats. Close your ears to his deceitful words of defeat.

You and I know a God who is bigger than our fears, and He has another plan. The ship may sink, but you are going to survive. Some of your cargo may need to be thrown overboard, but you won't drown.

What Paul said to those shackled, hungry prisoners, was also written for you: "Take courage. You're not going to die, but live!"

Today, there is a prophetic voice echoing from heaven above:

- "Mom, keep up your courage!"
- "Dad, keep up your courage!"
- "Teenager, keep up your courage!"

Be determined to keep the fear of despair and

depression from creeping in and taking up residence. The Lord will send someone to come alongside you with words of encouragement: "I believe in you and am holding you up in prayer. Stay strong!"

In my mind's eye I can see the relief that must have washed over the faces of the prisoners when Paul declared those God-given words of positive expectation. Without question they were fearful of the unknown, but they were fortified by the apostle's declarations of faith and power. Now they were thinking, "Thank God, someone is speaking life, speaking purpose and destiny in this situation."

THE CLOUDS WILL BREAK

We cannot avoid hardships and trouble, but as believers we need to embrace the strengths storms can produce. How much better to know that when misfortune strikes, you are going to endure—and when the clouds finally break you will be stronger.

Make a vow to your Creator that you will not be swayed, moved, or consumed, but will claim these words of Solomon: *"...the righteous stand firm forever"* (Proverbs 10:25).

Our foundation is not dependant on our limited human ability, but in the power of God's Son. As expressed in this beloved hymn:

> *My hope is built on nothing less*
> *Than Jesus' blood and righteousness;*
> *I dare not trust the sweetest frame,*
> *But wholly lean on Jesus' name.*
> *On Christ, the solid Rock, I stand;*
> *All other ground is sinking sand.*

Please allow me to pray these life-changing words with you today:

> *Lord, by Your Spirit, fill this child of Yours with courage. We break the spirit of fear, worry, anxiety, and stress. Lord, I pray in Jesus' name that You will fill this person with a spirit of daring and determination. May they take their eyes off of the wind, the rain, and refuse to listen to any negative forecast of the enemy. I pray they will hear Your still small voice speak to their spirit today, "Keep up your courage. You're going to make it."*

6
WISDOM
FOR FRIENDS

He who walks with the wise grows
wise, but a companion of fools suffers harm.

— P ROVERBS 1 3 : 2 0

It has been said, "Show me the people you hang around with and I'll show you the person you will become."

Are your present relationships helping to bring you to the destiny, the purpose, and the miracle God has prepared just for you? Are your friends speaking words of life, words of hope and healing?

In our key scripture, Solomon tells us that the man or woman who spends their time with fools *"suffers harm. "* In the original Hebrew, those two words mean "destruction"—and also "to screech, to cry at the top of your lungs."

When you surround yourself with negative individuals who are not wise, uplifting, or inspiring, your soul is screaming out, "Help! I'm drowning in a sea of negativity—by people who are not emotionally or spiritually healthy. They are dysfunctional!"

As the noted British theologian and writer, C. S. Lewis, observed, "The next best thing to being wise oneself is to live in a circle of those who are."

A LIFE-CHANGING DECISION

There is a marvelous story in the New Testament that illustrates the impact of the people with whom we associate.

It's about a man who was paralyzed, but he made a determined decision that he wasn't going to spend the rest of his life in that helpless condition.

One day Jesus visited the city of Capernaum. When the residents heard the news that He would be teaching at a certain home, a huge throng showed up. Scripture records:

So many gathered that there was no room left, not even outside the door, and he preached the word to them. Some men came, bringing to him a paralytic, carried by four of them. Since they could not get him to Jesus because of the crowd, they made an opening in the roof above Jesus and, after digging through it, lowered the mat the paralyzed man was lying on.

When Jesus saw their faith, he said to the paralytic, "Son, your sins are forgiven."

Now some teachers of the law were sitting there, thinking to themselves, "Why does this fellow talk like that? He's blaspheming! Who can forgive sins but God alone?"

Immediately Jesus knew in his spirit that this was what they were thinking in their hearts, and he said to them, "Why are you thinking these things? Which is easier: to say to the paralytic, 'Your sins are forgiven,' or to say, 'Get up, take your mat and walk'? But I want you to know that the Son of Man has authority on earth to forgive sins."

So he said to the man, "I tell you, get up, take your mat and go home." He got up, took his mat and walked out in full view of them all. This amazed everyone and they praised God, saying, "We have never seen anything like this!" (Mark 2:1-12).

This miracle occurred in Capernaum, which means "a place of comfort."

When you choose to be in the company of godly,

75

wise, encouraging men and women, you enter into a zone of peace and satisfaction.

What a comfort and joy to know you have friends you can trust and confide in—those with whom you can open up your heart and reveal the nagging fears and worries that are causing you stress and anxiety.

STRATEGIC CHOICES

This immobilized man could not even crawl to that house of miracles on his own; he needed the strong arms of others to help bring him to the Son of God.

I don't believe he randomly picked just anyone who was available, as we casually do sometimes in our relationships. He probably began thinking about his plan of action from the moment he heard Jesus was coming to his city. And when that day arrived, he no doubt thought, "This is my moment! This is what God wants me to do."

He was smart enough to understand that in his own strength, he was doomed to a life of being dependant on the kindness of others. He wasn't just taken to the home by one or two friends, but he strategically picked out *four* men to carry him to Jesus.

There's probably nothing supernatural in the number "four," but he chose men who were not only physically capable of lifting his stretcher, but also of lifting his spirits.

In reading this account in Acts, it struck me that for every encouragement God sends our way, the enemy plans a counter-attack. These are barriers that Satan places in our path to keep us from our miracle.

FOUR OBSTACLES

When you decide to step out in faith and move toward your healing, blessing, or what you are believing God for, there will be opposition ahead. Here are four roadblocks this man confronted that may also challenge you:

The First Obstacle: A Mental or Spiritual Barrier

Does God want me to have a purpose in this life? Does He want to use me for His kingdom? Is my heavenly Father content with me remaining paralyzed (in body or in mind), or does He want me to move forward?

In this biblical story, the mental and spiritual barriers were the most difficult this man had to overcome—and he met them head-on. I believe that as he was lying there on his mat, his body may not have been mobile, but in his mind he was doing cartwheels! His spirit was telling him, "God wants to heal you and make you whole. The Lord desires for you to have a specific purpose and destiny."

He did not wallow in despair; he believed and overcame the first roadblock.

The Second Obstacle: The Barrier of the Crowd

The house where Jesus was teaching was far too small for the throng that wanted to be near Him. To this paralyzed man, a party of one, the physical limitations of the situation may have seemed impossible to overcome.

When you are all alone and the crowd is so huge, you may question, "How on earth could I possibly see this Miracle Worker—let alone get close to Him?"

This is when doubt sets in. Perhaps you have faced such an overwhelming problem and thought:

- "I can't because _____ (fill in the blank)."
- "I believe God wants me to do this, but _____."
- "It might be a good idea, however, _____."

When you are supported by friends who are

people of destiny, you have the force, the power, to break through any barricade of the devil.

The Third Obstacle: Getting Through the Roof

When the four men bearing the weight of the infirmed man finally reached the crowded house, they could have easily surveyed the scene and told him, "Sorry, this is probably as far as we can go. We're tired, so let's just turn around and go home."

Instead, these four individuals were men of faith and purpose. They declared, "We have come this far—and we're not giving up! We will find a way!"

As Scripture records, *"...they made an opening in the roof above Jesus and, after digging through it, lowered the mat the paralyzed man was lying on"* (Mark 2:4).

These four stretcher-bearers literally cut a large hole in the roof in order to lower the paralytic where Christ was—the One who is the bearer of *all* our burdens.

There are times when we may only be a few feet away from experiencing a miracle, but we've grown weary, not willing to work, not ready to dig and fight.

Remember, the Bible tells us, *"For as the body without the spirit is dead, so faith without works is dead also"* (James 2:28 NKJV).

Our good deeds or personal efforts do not earn us

God's grace or His forgiveness, but when you are going after something you are believing the Lord for, it takes more than a nonchalant attitude.

The Fourth Obstacle: the Barrier of Religion

After breaking through the mental and physical barricades, a problem arose they didn't expect. As the man was lowered through the roof and was now lying in front of the Lord, Scripture tells us, *"When Jesus saw their faith, he said to the paralytic, 'Son, your sins are forgiven'"* (Mark 2:5).

Please notice that the Lord saw *"their"* faith—not just the hope and belief of the infirmed man, but also that of the four men who carried the mat, cut the roof, and lowered him down.

Immediately, a "religious spirit" surfaced. *"Some teachers of the law were sitting there, thinking to themselves, 'Why does this fellow talk like that? He's blaspheming! Who can forgive sins but God alone?'"* (verses 6-7). They began to challenge Jesus with questions and accusations.

In our lives, one of the most formidable barriers keeping us from the blessings of heaven are so-called spiritual people who piously tell us, "That's not the way we do things. God can't do that!"

Sadly, religion clings to rules and regulations. If

that's all people have as an anchor, they don't know how to respond when they see faith in action.

At that moment, Jesus knew in His spirit exactly what the critics were thinking in their hearts. He responded, *"Why are you thinking these things? Which is easier: to say to the paralytic, 'Your sins are forgiven,' or to say, 'Get up, take your mat and walk'? But I want you to know that the Son of Man has authority on earth to forgive sins"* (verses 8-1-0).

I pray you will not allow legalistic religion to keep you from the awesome future God has on your horizon.

WHO RECEIVES THE PRAISE?

This story ends with Jesus not only forgiving the man's sins, but totally healing his body. The paralytic *"got up, took his mat and walked out in full view of them all. This amazed everyone and they praised God, saying, 'We have never seen anything like this!'"* (verse 12).

I believe from that moment on—for the rest of his life—every time someone saw this healthy man, God received glory. This is the same with you and me. When we do great things for the Lord, our heavenly Father will openly receive the honor and praise.

This is all possible because we are willing, with faith and trust in the Lord, to overcome the obstacles placed in our paths.

LOOK FOR THESE!

Let me recommend four kinds of individuals with whom you need to surround yourself:

1. *People with high ethics* — men and women of stellar character, integrity and high morality, who you can trust and rely upon.

2. *People of experience* — who have "been there, done that," and will speak into your life with practical wisdom.

3. *People who elevate you* — who are pulling you up and lifting you to higher ground.

4. *People of encouragement* — who are supportive with their confidence, optimism, and inspiration.

Right now, think of some of your closest friends. Do they have and put into practice these four values and characteristics?

WHO TO AVOID

While we're on the topic, let me name four toxic voices—foolish men and women you should avoid at all cost.

1. *Small Thinkers* — these myopic people never see the big picture. If the roof is just one inch thick, they complain, "We will never be able to cut through it!" Avoid individuals who are motivated by doubt. We serve a mighty God, so start thinking that way!

2. *Skeptics* — men and women who always see the glass half empty instead of half full. Their focus is on the barriers, not on Jesus. I want friends who are looking up, not down!

3. *The Self-Righteous* — those whose conversation is filled with spiritual jargon, but they fail to walk the walk. In many cases, their "Praise the Lord," and "Hallelujah" vocabulary may be an attempt to compensate for what they lack in their hearts and souls.

4. *Suckers* — people who are stealing your God-given purpose. These are the joy-suckers and faith-suckers who are constantly draining the life right out of you.

If you are running with a crowd that has these toxic voices, now is the time to cut the ties. Otherwise you'll end up spiritually incapacitated and never receive your miracle.

CHOOSE DREAMERS AND DOERS

Look around and make an assessment of your close friends and confidants.

Far too frequently, I see believers whose sins have been forgiven, but they are paralyzed mentally, and physically. They're in a zone where instead of moving forward, they are stagnant and stale, merely existing.

I refuse to spend the rest of my life in such limbo. Instead, I am determined to surround myself with wise, godly people who speak life, health, and purpose to my soul.

Many find themselves in a co-dependent, dysfunctional relationship where they support or enable another persons's addiction, immaturity, poor mental health, under-achievement, irresponsibility, etc. On the surface it may seem inviting and safe—especially if it is an individual you have been around for many years.

If any of the above describes you, take a long, hard, introspective look at your situation. Is this a person who is going to help lead you to your destiny? Perhaps it is time to find a certified Christian counselor who can offer you some sound advice and guidance.

This very day, the Lord may be challenging you to cut off certain relationships that have been dragging you down rather than propelling you forward.

In the words of Edmund Jennings Lee, a prominent early American attorney, "Surround yourself with dreamers, and the doers, the believers and the thinkers, but most of all surround yourself with those who see the greatness within you even when you don't see it yourself."

Walk with the wise!

7

WISDOM FOR CORRECTION

He who listens to a life-giving rebuke will be at home among the wise. He who ignores discipline despises himself, but whoever heeds correction gains understanding.

– PROVERBS 15:31-32

When was the last time you were corrected? Was it as a child, a teenager, an adult? How long has it been since God used someone to suggest a possible improvement to your life? How did you respond? Did, like so many others, you become offended, upset, or perhaps thought of getting even?

For most people, the initial reaction is to become discouraged, defensive, or display outright rejection.

Since our heavenly Father loves us more than words can describe, there will be times when He disciplines His children for their good—so that His holiness, righteousness, and peace will shine through us.

There is a powerful passage in the book of Hebrews that can help open our eyes regarding how we should respond to correction.

We are told: *"And you have forgotten that word of encouragement that addresses you as sons: 'My son, do not make light of the Lord's discipline, and do not lose heart when he rebukes you, because the Lord disciplines those he loves, and he punishes everyone he accepts as a son'"* (Hebrews 12:5-6).

THREE RESPONSES

In these verses there are three specific options mentioned as to how we react to discipline:

Response #1: We Forget

The first words to circle in the above text are *"you have forgotten."*

Some people find it easy to say, "Oh, that slipped my mind"—especially if it has to do with putting into practice a task that takes self-control or personal effort.

But what about the tugging of the Holy Spirit on our conscience or the still small voice of God telling us to change our ways? Sadly, we often ignore what the Lord is trying to do through His correction.

This is why our heavenly Father continues to

remind us, "Don't forget!"

God is trying to impart His righteousness into us through a life-giving rebuke. It is for our benefit that we pay attention to His will and His direction.

Response #2: We Try to Make Light of It

The second group of words I want you to underline in the above passage are these: *"do not make light."*

An order from the throne of heaven should never be taken lightly, or shrugged off casually with, "Oh, God must be trying to tell my spouse or someone else. Surely, that's not for me!"

God's correction is serious business.

Response #3: We Lose Heart

Next, highlight the words, *"do not lose heart."*

It is human nature that when we're disciplined, we become discouraged. This is why some mistakenly think, "God is mad at me. He must not love me"—and their spirits begin to sink.

Just the opposite! A tap on the shoulder from your heavenly Father is a sign that He is paying attention to your daily walk and cares for you more than you can ever imagine.

The Making of a Son or Daughter

Solomon lets us know that we will be *"among the wise"* if we listen *"to a life-giving rebuke"* (Proverbs 15:31).

This truth is echoed in the New Testament by the writer of Hebrews, who tells us:

Endure hardship as discipline; God is treating you as sons. For what son is not disciplined by his father? If you are not disciplined (and everyone undergoes discipline), then you are illegitimate children and not true sons.

Moreover, we have all had human fathers who disciplined us and we respected them for it. How much more should we submit to the Father of our spirits and live. Our fathers disciplined us for a little while as they thought best; but God disciplines us for our good, that we may share in his holiness.

No discipline seems pleasant at the time, but painful. Later on, however, it produces a harvest of righteousness and peace for those who have been trained by it.

Therefore, strengthen your feeble arms and weak knees. "Make level paths for your feet," so that the lame may not be disabled, but rather healed (Hebrews 12:7-13).

Wow! Correction and discipline confirms that we are true sons and daughters of the Most High. Sure, it can be humbling, even painful at times, but it is soon forgotten when we reap a bumper crop of righteousness and peace!

So thank God for His rebuke. Flex your spiritual muscles, lift up your head, and start moving forward!

YOUR CATEGORY?

If you had to place yourself in one of the following groups, which one best describes you?

- *The Wise* – love and pursue correction.
- *The Growing* – appreciate correction, but at times begrudgingly accept it.
- *The Simple* – open-minded, but indifferent towards correction.
- *The Fools* – annoyed by correction.
- *The Scoffers* – hate correction.

How you respond determines your future.

The Warning

In chapter 2, when we discussed what Solomon had to say regarding "Wisdom for Temptation." A prime example was David and his sin with Bathsheba.

However, there is more to the story, especially regarding how God rebuked David and was not about to let him get away with his transgression.

Instead, the Lord was so concerned over David's behavior that He placed a man in his path to bring a heavenly reprimand. As it is written, *"The Lord sent Nathan to David"* (2 Samuel 12:1).

How many times have you wandered off course, yet you knew God was so concerned that He would not allow you to totally fail. Even though you didn't want to admit your faults, the Lord sent an individual to give you the signal, "Stop! Turn around! Repent!"

Think for a moment and recall how this has happened in your own life. The Lord sent a man or a woman with a stern message, yet you erected a barrier because you were insecure, fearful, or defensive. As a result, you rejected the Lord's warning to turn your life around

The person God chooses could be a teacher, an employer, a pastor, a television evangelist, or a relative. As the Good Shepherd, the Lord is protective of

His flock and will dispatch someone because He cares enough to bring admonishment. The reason this is necessary is because God wants you to walk in His pre-ordained destiny.

Through Nathan, the Lord brought correction into David's life. How he responded, however, determined David's next steps.

Today, the directive God is sending may come from:

- A Facebook page you look at.
- A message you hear from the pulpit.
- An email you receive.
- A passage of Scripture you read.

Through often unexpected sources, the Lord is sending a message that He is not about to let you wander down the wrong path.

A TOTAL TRANSFORMATION

The name "Nathan" means "giver." This is significant considering God was in the process of presenting David with a life-giving rebuke.

Maybe, just maybe, God said, "Nathan, I need to send you to warn David because he's at a crossroads and could turn one way or the other.

Thankfully, after Nathan chastised David (2 Samuel 121-7), David came to his senses and responded, *"I have sinned against the Lord"* (verse 10).

From that moment forward, David's legacy was changed because he responded properly to the correction given by God through His servant, Nathan.

Later, as an aftermath of this confrontation, David wrote this psalm:

> *Have mercy on me, O God, according to your unfailing love; according to your great compassion blot out my transgressions. Wash away all my iniquity and cleanse me from my sin. For I know my transgressions, and my sin is always before me. Against you, you only, have I sinned and done what is evil in your sight, so you are right in your verdict when you speak and justified when you judge...*
>
> *Cleanse me with hyssop, and I will be clean; wash me, and I will be whiter than snow...*
>
> *Create in me a pure heart, O God, and renew a steadfast spirit within me. Do not cast me from your presence or take your Holy Spirit from me...*
>
> *Deliver me from the guilt of bloodshed, O God, you who are God my Savior, and my*

tongue will sing of your righteousness...
*My sacrifice, O God, is a broken spirit; a
broken and contrite heart you, God, will not
despise"* (Psalm 51:1-4, 7,10-11,14,17).

What a beautiful, life-defining moment. David is
not defensive or blaming others. Instead of making
excuses, he is asking God for cleansing and forgiveness. In total repentance, he told the Lord, "Against
You, and You alone I have sinned."

Then he asked God to renew his joy and revive his
spirit. What a heart-felt prayer!

ARE YOU READY TO "MAN UP"?

There will be times when you might not like the
message, or even the messenger, but God will intro-
duce into your life a person who will give a rebuke
that can have a direct bearing on your destiny.

I pray you will have the heart and wisdom of David
to admit your mistakes, ask God for His forgiveness,
and say, "Lord, I'm ready for an about-face. Help me
to be more like You."

In many respects, your future depends on how you
respond to the "Nathans" in your life.

Do you have what it takes to admit, "It's not the

fault of my parents, my kindergarten teacher, my pastor, or the president"? Are you man or woman enough to confess, "Lord, I am to blame—and I am repenting"?

God is merciful. He will hear your cry and forgive you.

Who is Being Sent?

Here are some "Nathans" who will cross your path to give you life-giving correction.

1. God
The ultimate authority to get you back on track is your Creator.

He declares, *"Those whom I love I rebuke and discipline. So be earnest, and repent. Here I am! I stand at the door and knock. If anyone hears my voice and opens the door, I will come in and eat with him, and he with me"* (Revelation 3:19-20).

2. Spiritual Leaders
Paul the Apostle gave this advice to his spiritual son, Timothy: *"In the presence of God and of Christ Jesus, who will judge the living and the dead, and in view of his appearing and his kingdom, I give you this*

95

charge: Preach the Word; be prepared in season and out of season; correct, rebuke and encourage--with great patience and careful instruction" (2 Timothy 4:1-2).

3. Your Parents, Your Family

God has given mothers and fathers authority to provide much-needed correction. As Solomon writes, *"Folly is bound up in the heart of a child, but the rod of discipline will drive it far from him"* (Proverbs 22:15).

4. Friends

The advice you need may come from an individual who is very close to you. As it is written, *"It is better to heed a wise man's rebuke than to listen to the song of fools"* (Ecclesiastes 7:5).

5. Employers

Instead of looking at your boss as an enemy, perhaps he or she has been placed in a position of authority to give you an admonition that mirrors God's intent.

Scripture tells us, *"Slaves, obey your earthly masters with respect and fear, and with sincerity of heart, just as you would obey Christ. Obey them not*

*only to win their favor when their eye is on you, but
like slaves of Christ, doing the will of God from your
heart"* (Ephesians 6:5-6).

5. Leaders in Authority

The Bible is clear regarding the fact that we are to
obey the rulers of government that have been placed
in charge of our cities, states, and nations.

Specifically, God's Word tells us: *"Remind the
people to be subject to rulers and authorities, to be
obedient, to be ready to do whatever is good, to
slander no one, to be peaceable and considerate,
and to show true humility toward all men"* (Titus
3:1-2).

YOUR RESPONSE

When your heavenly Father sees fit to correct you,
I pray you will respond like David—not being
defensive, but humbly say, "God, it's You and You
alone I have sinned against. Create in me a clean
heart. Help me to accept this chastisement from
You."

This is walking with the wise. God is not trying to
harm or wound us, but to give us life!

When the "Nathans" are sent your way, please do

not be too proud or tempted to discard their warning. Remember, they have been ordered by your heavenly Father to stop you in your tracks so you will take a long hard look at your behavior and make a change for the better. In the process of making you *holy,* God wants to make you *whole!*

Remember the sage advice of King Solomon: *"Whoever heeds correction gains understanding"* (Proverbs 15:32).

Discipline produces wisdom!

8

WISDOM FOR YOUR DESTINY

In his heart a man plans his course,
but the Lord determines his steps.

— P R O V E R B S   1 6 : 9

When Solomon wrote the words, *"a man plans his course,"* he was fully aware that each of us have our own ideas, agenda, and game plan for life. This is based on the fact that we were created with a free will to make personal choices. However, there is a divine, ultimate destiny that was mapped out for you before you were ever born.

This key verse concludes with: *"...the Lord determines his steps"* —that is God's will, and we can only be successful if we walk His path.

In construction, architectural engineers create a blueprint to help the bricklayers, carpenters, electricians, and everyone involved with the building process to stay on track. Solomon reminds us that even though we may think we are in control, God is the Architect, and He is the one who will order our steps.

In the words of the psalmist, *"If the Lord delights in a man's way, he makes his steps firm; though he stumble, he will not fall, for the Lord upholds him with his hand"* (Psalm 37:23-24). And he prayed *"Direct my footsteps according to your word; let no sin rule over me"* (Psalm 119:133).

PUTTING GOD TO THE TEST

Have you ever stood at a crossroads and felt confused as to what direction to take? Perhaps you asked God, "Do You want me to do this? What is Your will? I don't know whether to turn left or right. Lord, speak to me; I need Your guidance."

Written in the Old Testament is the story of a man who faced the same dilemma. His name is Gideon, which means "warrior."

However, when he encountered the army of the Midianites, he didn't feel like a brave champion. He was unsure and indecisive. Gideon was questioning, "Okay God, I think You want me to go to battle against these people, but are You sure? Let me put You to a test."

According to Scripture, here is what Gideon told God:

"If you will save Israel by my hand as you have promised—look, I will place a wool fleece on the threshing floor. If there is dew only on the fleece and all the ground is dry, then I will know that you will save Israel by my hand, as you said."

And that is what happened. Gideon rose early the next day; he squeezed the fleece and wrung out the dew—a bowlful of water.

Then Gideon said to God, "Do not be angry with me. Let me make just one more request. Allow me one more test with the fleece, but this time make the fleece dry and let the ground be covered with dew."

That night God did so. Only the fleece was dry; all the ground was covered with dew" (Judges 6:36-40).

This particular story is in the Bible for a reason, and it provided a confirmation regarding a specific circumstance. While there are times when we, like Gideon, need to throw out a fleece, we can't go through life making decisions based on whether or not the Lord is going to honor our "test."

There are many other options.

EIGHT TOOLS FOR KNOWING GOD'S WILL

Scripture opens our understanding to several ways you can know the purpose God has planned for your future. Let me share eight tools you can use:

Tool #1: Opened and Closed Doors

"What he opens no one can shut, and what he shuts no one can open" (Revelation 3:7).

There are times you feel as though you are standing in front of an entryway, not knowing what is on the other side. That's when you need to pray, "God, if this is not Your will, I want You to close the door." Or, "Lord, if this is what You want me to do, please show me by allowing this door to open."

Tool #2: Wise Counsel

"Pride only breeds quarrels, but wisdom is found in those who take advice" (Proverbs 13:10). *"For lack of guidance a nation falls, but many advisers make victory sure"* (Proverbs 11:14).

What a thrill to be at a point of decision and know you have been blessed with friends to whom you can turn for godly advice.

There are certain individuals you can grab a bite to

eat with, and in confidence let them know, "Hey, this is what's going on. I need your help and guidance."

The Lord has placed them in your path as one of the means of revealing His will.

Tool #3: The Holy Spirit

"But when he, the Spirit of truth, comes, he will guide you into all truth. He will not speak on his own; he will speak only what he hears, and he will tell you what is yet to come" (John 16:13).

The one thing we need when we are trying to discern God's direction is truth—and this is where the Holy Spirit plays a crucial role. It's not just that He guides you, but He will lead you to the right objective.

Be sensitive to Him, keeping in mind that the Spirit does not use force to push His way into your life. He is a gentleman who must be asked and invited.

With humility, say, "Holy Spirit, I need Your direction. Lead me into all truth." He will be your trusted Counselor, your Guide.

You'll know you are on course when you begin to notice that each of these tools are lining up per-fectly—they are in unison.

Tool #4: God's Word

"Your word is a lamp to my feet and a light for my

path" (Psalm 119:105).

I've learned to be grateful for flashlights! On a "guys" fishing trip to Montana, we were staying in a RV at a campground when, in the middle of the night, I needed to go to the restroom—which was about a half mile away. It was dark and scary, and there were bears prowling in the woods. I'm so thankful that Tammi reminded me before I left, "Be sure to take a flashlight."

That pitch-black night, I'm glad I listened to my wife!

Our heavenly Father does not want any of His children to be alone or afraid on their journey through life, so He has provided a lamp for your feet and a light for your path—His Word.

When you are having to make a critical decision (and I don't mean what flavor of coffee you're going to drink in the morning), open the pages of Scripture and be ready to receive divine wisdom. You'll find it is like a spotlight from heaven shining on the road you're traveling, illuminating the path ahead.

Tool #5: Discerning His Voice

"Whether you turn to the right or to the left, your ears will hear a voice behind you, saying, 'This is the way; walk in it'" (Isaiah 30:21).

God leads in one of two ways through His audible voice:

One: He will be behind you, giving you direction.
Two: There will be times when He is in front of you, asking you to follow where He leads.

I wish I could promise that the Lord is always going to be ahead of you, saying," Follow Me," and showing you the safe path to take. But often He is in the background, and you have to live by faith.

Perhaps you have been at a moment of decision and you hear Him telling you, "Turn left," "Turn, right," "Go straight ahead," or "Stand still."

As believers, we need to have discernment and a sensitivity to know that whether He is leading us or behind us, we clearly hear His voice. Always keep an open heart and a receptive ear for the time God utters the reassuring words, "This is the way; walk in it."

Remember, Christ is our Shepherd and we are His sheep. As such, He made this incredible statement: *"My sheep listen to my voice; I know them, and they follow me"* (John 10:27).

Are you listening? Can you discern His voice? Are you following?

Tool #6: God's Peace

"Let the peace of Christ rule in your hearts, since as members of one body you were called to peace. And be thankful" (Colossians 3:15).

That word *"rule"* means to umpire or to arbitrate. This is what takes place in a baseball game, when the official standing behind home plate is calling balls and strikes.

In this verse, Paul the Apostle is telling us that when we are faced with a serious choice, we need to let the peace of God be the confirmation as to whether it is the Lord's will, or not.

Have you ever been ready to make a decision and yet something just doesn't feel right? You're uneasy. That is the peace of God within you, umpiring—"No. Don't do it!"

Speaking through the prophet Isaiah, the Lord tells us, *"You will go out in joy and be led forth in peace"* (Isaiah 55:12).

When you are about to make a choice and can honestly admit, "I have a green light; a peace about this," that's all you need to know.

Tool #7: Confirmation

"But if he will not listen, take one or two others along, so that every matter may be established by the

testimony of two or three witnesses" (Matthew 18:16).

On matters that may be contentious, God's will can be determined when it is verified by others—in this case by more than one witness.

However, make certain that those involved with the decision-making are men and women of the highest integrity, who are spiritually sound and faithful believers.

Tool #8: The Prophetic Voice

"Do not put out the Spirit's fire; do not treat prophecies with contempt. Test everything. Hold on to the good. Avoid every kind of evil" (1 Thessalonians 5:19-22).

There will be times in your walk here on earth that God will bring a prophetic voice to speak to you. When that takes place, have a receptive heart to receive the message. As the Apostle Paul writes, *"Do not put out the Spirit's fire."*

It's so easy to dismiss listening to the voice of a person with "A word from the Lord" as a crazy lunatic trying to inflate his or her ego by claiming to hear directly from God about you! However, be very careful. The Bible informs us, *"Christ himself gave the apostles, the prophets, the evangelists, the pastors and teachers, to equip his people for works of service, so*

107

the body of Christ may be built up" (Ephesians 4:11).

You may not fully understand it, but when you are at a turning point and you're not sure what to do, God will bring a prophetic voice into your life that will speak to you, "Thus saith the Lord!"

When the Lord uses that voice, it will confirm the direction God is giving you by other means.

Does it happen at every decision? No. But, there are times when we are in crisis mode and don't know where to turn. Let me ask you to open your heart and say, "Holy Spirit, if You want to give me direction, I will listen to what You say. Send me a prophet—a man or woman that I can trust. Let them speak into my life."

Often, the voice of a prophet will confirm what God has already said through His Word, through wise counsel, open and closed doors, and other ways.

There was a critical moment in my own life when I needed to know God's will for my future in ministry. I used all of the tools I have mentioned, and wrote the direction I was receiving in a small notebook.

Things seemed to be lining up, but still in doubt, I passionately prayed, "Lord, I want to know that I know that I know!"

I read where Paul wrote, *"Timothy, my son, I give you this instruction in keeping with the prophecies once made about you, so that by following them you may fight the good fight, holding on to faith"* (1 Timothy 1:18-19).

I claimed those words for me.

At the point where I had to make a final decision about my future, I cried out, "God, I need You to speak to me."

Over time, one by one, He began to send prophets my way—individuals whom I trusted. And I wrote what they said in my notebook. The answers God gave me all fell into place and I stepped out in faith.

Were there moments of trials and discouragement? Of course. But every time I was tired or ready to throw in the towel, I opened up my book of handwritten notes and was inspired to take one more step of faith.

There may come a day when God will call you to do something extraordinary and you will have to battle the gates of hell. It is with these prophecies that you fight the good fight. I can tell you from personal experience that they are like a flaming sword that enables you to have the fire and passion to fulfill whatever God asks of you.

A "Straight Line" Answer

I want you to remember that the unique purpose God has for you needs to be confirmed by more than one of the tools I have presented. When they merge together and form a straight line, you can be assured that you are in God's perfect will.

Please pray these words with me:

Lord, I have my ideas, plans, and agenda, but let me recognize that You are the Architect who is going to direct my steps and lead me on the right path.

Reveal what You want me to do, because my life is not my own. It is Yours. For that reason I am praying, God, not my will, but Yours.

Today, the Lord is ready to provide His wisdom for your destiny.

9

WISDOM FOR A HAPPY HEART

A merry heart does good, like medicine,
but a broken spirit dries the bones.
— PROVERBS 17:22 NKJV

Life is a journey, enjoy the ride!

Every day, take a few minutes to have a little fun and let your hair down. After all, on earth we have only one life; this is it!

Many in the church are a bit too serious, too stoic, too conservative in their outlook and expressions. It's okay to remind ourselves of the words of Solomon, that *"a merry heart does good—like medicine."*

Talk show host Dennis Prager, author of *Happiness is a Serious Problem,* made this observation: "Unhappy, let alone angry, religious people provide more persuasive arguments for atheism and secularism than do all the arguments of atheists."

Now that's quite an indictment of the church!

So as Christians, we need to lighten up! Instead of

111

scowling and telling people what you're against, try smiling and letting the world know what you are *for*.

When was the last time you laughed? I mean really *belly*-laughed? How long has it been since you could look in the mirror and say, "I'm enjoying life. I am really having fun!"?

I know life can be stressful, and I am not trying to avoid reality, but since Solomon gives us a "merry heart" prescription," we had better pay attention.

That word *merry* means "bright"—which reminds me of the words of Jesus, who said, *"Let your light shine"* (Matthew 5:16).

When you're shining, it's contagious. People want to be around you—and through your very countenance you are giving glory to God.

On the other hand, failing to laugh has consequences—your very bones will shrivel and dry up!

PARACHUTES AND MONKEYS!

"Okay, Scott," you say, "make me smile." I'll give it a try.

A small private airplane lost its engine and was going down fast. There were four people on board and only three parachutes.

One guy hollered out, "I'm a heart surgeon. I've got 17 patients to see. I need a parachute. He strapped it on and jumped out.

The next man chimed in, "I'm the most intelligent person in the world. I am full of knowledge and I'm needed on earth." So he grabbed a parachute and jumped.

Now there were only two people left—a bishop and a 14-year-old boy. The bishop turned to the young man and graciously said, "Son, I've been around this world a long time, so I'm going to give you this last parachute."

The boy replied, "Don't worry about that. The smartest man in the world just grabbed my backpack!"

Can I tell you one more?

A young girl asked her mother, "Mom, where did I come from?"

The mother answered, "Well, you came from Adam and Eve."

The girl responded, "Okay. Is that it?"—and the mother took the opportunity to tell her about the birds and the bees.

The next day, she went to her father and

asked the same question, "Dad, where did I come from?"

He thought for a moment and answered, "Well, you came from the apes and the monkeys, and you evolved into what you are today."

She looked a little confused, so the following morning she went back to her mom, saying, "You told me I came from Adam and Eve, but dad tells me I came from a bunch of monkeys."

Her mother calmly told her daughter, "Well, your dad is right; but that's on his side of the family!"

EIGHT ENEMIES OF A MERRY HEART

Let me ask you a personal question: What are the triggers that make you grouchy, angry, or upset—that keep you from enjoying life to the fullest?

Allow me to share what I believe are eight enemies of a merry heart. These are joy-busters we need to avoid:

The First Enemy: Dealing With the Daily Stress of Life

Jesus, in the Sermon on the Mount, addressed what

we become anxious about; things that weigh on our hearts and keep us from relishing life.

When you feel that you are about to drown in a sea of stress I recommend that you read these words of the Son of God. Let them sink deep into your spirit:

Do not worry about your life, what you will eat or drink; or about your body, what you will wear. Is not life more important than food, and the body more important than clothes? Look at the birds of the air; they do not sow or reap or store away in barns, and yet your heavenly Father feeds them. Are you not much more valuable than they?

Who of you by worrying can add a single hour to his life? And why do you worry about clothes? See how the lilies of the field grow. They do not labor or spin. Yet I tell you that not even Solomon in all his splendor was dressed like one of these.

If that is how God clothes the grass of the field, which is here today and tomorrow is thrown into the fire, will he not much more clothe you, O you of little faith?

So do not worry, saying, '"What shall we eat?" or "What shall we drink?"'or "What shall we wear?" For the pagans run after all these

> *things, and your heavenly Father knows that you need them. But seek first his kingdom and his righteousness, and all these things will be given to you as well.*
>
> *Therefore do not worry about tomorrow, for tomorrow will worry about itself. Each day has enough trouble of its own* (Matthew 6:25-34).

Every time I read this passage, I get convicted; I get inspired; it helps me become a lot less stressed.

Jesus is saying to each of us, "Don't worry!"

The Second Enemy: Looking Down

Walking through the mall the other day, it suddenly hit me: practically everybody was either texting on their cell phone or clicking their iPad. They were navigating through life *looking down!*

This is not only dangerous, it's life-threatening. Government statistics reveal that in the U.S. more than 3,300 are killed and over 400,000 are injured each year on our highways because of distracted drivers. This should come as no surprise since more than 200 *billion* text messages were sent or received in our country alone.

How sad. In most cases, when we look down, all we see are our problems and the impossible situations we face. If we spend our lives with eyes that are lowered, we will miss the heavenly perspective that is only gained by lifting our hearts and looking up. This is why we are told, *"Since, then, you have been raised with Christ, set your hearts on things above, where Christ is seated at the right hand of God. Set your minds on things above, not on earthly things"* (Colossians 3:1-2).

Your Creator is not extending His arm and pushing your head down so you will live in the trenches. Instead, you need to say with the psalmist, *"But you, Lord, are the shield around me; my glory, the One who lifts my head high"* (Psalm 3:3).

When you exhibit that kind of attitude, it's like God's aspirin, bringing the positive into your heart and life. Yes, it is truly medicine for the soul.

The Third Enemy: Surrounding Yourself With Dull People

If we are to shine brightly, what's the point of hanging around those who are dull? The real problem is that their boring, ho-hum personalities can rub off on you!

The Bible cautions, *"Do not be misled: 'Bad company corrupts good character.' Come back to your senses as you ought, and stop sinning"* (1 Corinthians 15:33).

The reason Paul uses the word "misled," is because

we can easily be led astray by associating with the wrong people. Even more serious, when we do, we are actually *sinning!* Why? Because they are corrupting us and dragging us down to their level.

It makes sense to chose a circle of friends who sparkle and shine. After being with them you feel encouraged, inspired, and ready to climb to higher ground.

The Fourth Enemy: Not Having a Contented Spirit

In a world where the media is constantly pushing the sale of new products that are bigger and better, it's easy to become upset that we're not "keeping up with the Jonses."

The reason the tenth commandment says, *"You shall not covet"* (Exodus 20:17) is because God knows how quickly we can become unhappy with our lot in life.

Instead, we need to be like Paul the Apostle, who told the believers at Philippi, "*I have learned to be content whatever the circumstances. I know what it is to be in need, and I know what it is to have plenty. I have learned the secret of being content in any and every situation, whether well fed or hungry, whether living in plenty or in want. I can do everything through Christ who gives me strength"* (Philippians 4:11-13).

Many quote the words, "I can do all things through Christ," believing God for a bigger house, a faster car, or increased income. But they leave off the rest of the verse that tells us it is Christ who gives us the strength to be content.

Paul found the secret of true fulfillment.

When I'm around those who are anxious to get a promotion, or pushing to acquire more, I rarely get a vibe of happiness. They are "driven" people, but by the wrong motives.

My wife's grandma is a tremendous saint of God who has passed her 90th birthday and has dementia. Every time we go to visit her it is such a joy. She doesn't know what's going on, but I bring my iPad because she loves to watch the old Shirley Temple movies. Suddenly, her face lights up as she engages in her childhood.

I can count on her saying, "Scott and Tammi, I'm content with whatever situation I am in." About 10 seconds later, she will repeat it again: "Scott and Tammi, I'm content with whatever situation I am in."

We all need that serene, tranquil spirit surging through our hearts.

The Fifth Enemy: Comparing Ourselves to Other People

A major killjoy of a merry heart is measuring yourself by the lives of others, whether it is a friend you admire or a role model in sports or on the movie screen. Some people live their whole lives riddled with envy, trying to be someone else.

Jesus said you are to *"Love your neighbor as yourself"* (Matthew 22:19). To put it another way, how can you love someone else if you don't have love for YOU?

The Almighty is waiting for you to reach the place where you say with gratitude, "God, you have gifted me with talents and abilities, and I'm going to be who You created me to be. I will be uniquely me. I love what You have made and I'm not going to live my life comparing myself to my brother, my sister, or even my enemy."

Of course there are rough edges we need to smooth and refine, so measure your progress by how far you have come from where you started, not by the talents of another person.

The Sixth Enemy: Forgetting That We Are Just Passing Through This Earth

Every once in awhile we need to be reminded that

this life is not all there is. We are just passing through.

When the writer of Hebrews details the faith of Enoch, Noah, Abraham, and other saints of God, he says, they were *"strangers and pilgrims on the earth"* (Hebrews 11:13 NKJV). Then he adds, *"But now they desire a better...heavenly country...[and God] has prepared a city for them"* (verses 15-16).

Eternity is ahead.

In losing someone to death, as Christians we say that person "is with Jesus." But do we truly believe it?

My friend, if your loved ones accepted Christ as their Savior and Lord, they are rejoicing with Jesus right now, and we're going to join them one day.

When we finally awaken to the revelation that life is more than a family, a mortgage, and a career, everything changes. Just the thought of heaven should bring merriment to our minds, happiness to our hearts, and satisfaction to our souls.

The fact that you will spend forever with Jesus ought to put a big, broad smile on your face.

The words of the old hymn still ring true today:

> *When we all get to heaven,*
> *What a day of rejoicing that will be!*
> *When we all see Jesus,*
> *We'll sing and shout the victory!*

The Seventh Enemy: Always Focusing on Our Own Well Being, Not on Others

After years of helping untold thousands by establishing food banks and outreach centers for the needy, I can tell you that true joy comes through a commitment to service. This may include lending a hand to the homeless, providing a warm meal for the hungry, or going to bat for someone who is down and out.

As a Christian, serving others should be our way of life—regardless of whether those on the receiving end are rich or poor.

Paul spoke to this issue very clearly when he wrote, *"Make my joy complete by being like-minded, having the same love, being one in spirit and purpose. Do nothing out of selfish ambition or vain conceit, but in humility consider others better than yourselves. Each of you should look not only to your own interests, but also to the interests of others. Your attitude should be the same as that of Christ Jesus"* (Philippians 2:2-5).

Life is so much more than what you acquire or always looking out for "number one." Have a heart for others and enrich yours in the process.

The Eighth Enemy: Forgetting God's Will For Your Life

The reason Satan fires everything in his arsenal—arrows of doubt, discouragement, and defeat—is because he wants you to focus and worry over your problems, not your possibilities.

A sour, negative attitude portrays that it is all about "me, myself, and I."

With such a selfish outlook, is it any wonder that many struggle and often fail to find their God-given purpose?

If you want to see a dramatic change in your future, let me recommend that you read the following passage of Scripture not once, not twice, but again and again until it is etched in your memory: *"Be joyful always; pray continually; give thanks in all circumstances, for this is God's will for you in Christ Jesus"* (1 Thessalonians 5:16-18).

This is more than wisdom for a happy heart, it is the will of God for you.

10

WISDOM FOR CONFLICT

*An offended brother is more
unyielding than a fortified city, and disputes
are like the barred gates of a citadel.*

– PROVERBS 18:19

Life is filled with obstacle courses and stumbling blocks. The word, "offense" or "offended" actually means a trap. If you tick someone off, in some cases, get ready for that person to start digging a pit for you to fall into!

I've met individuals who have been highly offended and have never escaped the snare that was set for them. Their resentment and anger has lingered for years, even a lifetime! There are extreme situations where parents no longer talk to their kids over a perceived wrongdoing that to some may seem trivial.

God wants you to be liberated from that trap, and His Word will show you the key to becoming free.

None of us will make it through life without being rebuffed or shown some form of disrespect. There will be times when you're not going to see eye-to-eye with your spouse, your children, or your co-workers. You will be upset by hurtful words, and deeply wounded by the actions of others.

I'm glad that we don't have to look to Dr. Phil or Oprah for guidance on how to deal with being slighted or offended. God's Word is insightful and direct, and it gives us the wisdom we need.

Life Lessons for Conflict

The Bible is an amazing book. Not just because it shows us how to prepare for eternity, but it gives us principles to live by on earth.

One of the most practical lessons in Scripture deals with the topic of acceptable behavior and the proper attitude for those involved in conflict.

Here is the teaching:

> *Each of you must put off falsehood and speak truthfully to your neighbor, for we are all members of one body. "In your anger do not sin": Do not let the sun go down while you are still angry, and do not give the devil a foothold.*

Anyone who has been stealing must steal no longer, but must work, doing something useful with their own hands, that they may have something to share with those in need.

Do not let any unwholesome talk come out of your mouths, but only what is helpful for building others up according to their needs, that it may benefit those who listen. And do not grieve the Holy Spirit of God, with whom you were sealed for the day of redemption.

Get rid of all bitterness, rage and anger, brawling and slander, along with every form of malice. Be kind and compassionate to one another, forgiving each other, just as in Christ God forgave you (Ephesians 4:25-32).

TEN RULES OF ENGAGEMENT

When you delve into this passage, there is a wealth of advice regarding how to respond when you have been aggrieved or provoked to the point of anger.

On the other hand, perhaps it is you who has crossed the line between civility and contention. In either case, take a few steps back and consider using these Ten Rules of Engagement:

Rule #1: Be Real and Truthful

"Each of you must put off falsehood" (Ephesians 4:25).

It's useless to mask or avoid the issue, so the first step is to identify the problem. It's okay to admit, "I am upset—and here's the reason why."

The second step in overcoming an offense is to speak truthfully. This verse is telling us, "Get real!" It is perfectly in order for a man or woman to *"speak truthfully to his neighbor, for we are all members of one body"* (verse 25).

This may include a face-to-face encounter where you let your feelings be known: "You have made me very angry. But because we are brothers and sisters in Christ, I want to share my heart with you...and am asking you to do the same."

Remember, when you are offended it affects me, and when I am offended it affects you—because as believers we are all one family.

Rule #2: Be Righteous

"In your anger do not sin" (verse 26).

There's no law against being upset, even for the righteous, but make sure it does not escalate into sin.

It's a major problem to walk around boiling over with anger and rage, yet failing to confess it. We need to pray, "God, help me deal with this situation righteously. I want to do it Your way."

We've all had circumstances where we are guilty of doing it wrong, and because we didn't approach it biblically, things got muddled and it became a big, tangled mess.

Take the time to talk to the Lord in prayer about the conflict.

Rule #3: Be Quick

"Do not let the sun go down while you are still angry" (verse 26).

After a hard day, exhausted and upset, it is so easy to flop into bed and think, "I'll deal with this in the morning." But so often one night turns into two, then weeks, months, and years, because you did not quickly resolve what was bothering you.

When you ignore situations, they can quickly mushroom out of control. Your personality may be non-combative and you say, "Oh, just let it go. The problem is going to just magically disappear."

As we all know, life's not like that. If you turn a blind eye to any dispute, it can be magnified in a hot minute.

Face the issue head on and ask God for His help to walk through it.

Rule #4: Be Alert

"Do not give the devil a foothold" (verse 27).

Our enemy loves to use small, minor disagreements to cause big trouble. We must be aware of his schemes.

If you fail to come to terms with the person you're having a clash with, you are giving Satan the foothold he's looking for. Don't give him one inch inside the door to your heart. His foot will be followed by his hand, his elbow, and suddenly you're overwhelmed!

Be alert! If he gains access it can cause damage to your marriage, your business, and you spiritual walk.

Conflict began with the first family; Adam and Eve, and their two sons, Cain and Abel.

As we learn in Genesis 4, Cain was a farmer who worked the fields growing crops. Abel was a shepherd. When it was time for sacrificial worship, Cain brought fruit, and Abel presented a lamb.

Back in those days, God received sacrifices of a lamb or goat; so basically, the Lord told Cain his offering was not acceptable. He received Abel's sacrifice and rejected Cain's.

Scripture records, *"Cain was very angry, and his face was downcast. Then the Lord said to Cain, 'Why are you angry? Why is your face downcast? If you do what is right, will you not be accepted? But if you do not do what is right, sin is crouching at your door; it desires to have you, but you must master it'"* (Genesis 4:5-7).

Cain was so upset that while they were in the field, *"Cain attacked his brother Abel and killed him"* (verse 8).

Be watchful! Sin is lurking at your very door—and it can lead to death!

Rule #5: Be Busy

"He who has been stealing must steal no longer, but must work, doing something useful with his own hands, that he may have something to share with those in need" (Ephesians 4:28).

I am sure you've heard it said, "Idle hands are the devil's workshop." It's true! Perhaps this is why Solomon had so much to say about being industrious, including:

- *"Lazy hands make for poverty, but diligent hands bring wealth"* (Proverbs 10:4).
- *"All hard work brings a profit, but mere talk leads only to poverty"* (Proverbs 14:23).
- *"One who is slack in his work is brother to one who destroys"* (Proverbs 18:9).

When you are busy working, using the talents the Lord has gifted you with, you have the ability and privilege to give back—which is far better than being embroiled in hostility.

Rule #6: Be Wise

"Do not let any unwholesome talk come out of your mouths, but only what is helpful for building others up according to their needs, that it may benefit those who listen" (verse 29).

In dealing with any dispute, we must always guard our words. What we say can never be taken back.

I like the observation of author Orson Scott Card: "Among my most prized possessions are the words I have never spoken."

This topic is especially critical in our digital world, where your comments can be spread across the globe in a matter of seconds.

When you feel anger stirring inside, ask God for wisdom to keep your emotions in check.

Rule #7: Be Sensitive

"Do not grieve the Holy Spirit of God" (verse 30).

It may sound simplistic, but hurting people hurt others!

There are times in dealing with men and women

that I ask myself, "Where in the world did that come from? Could it be that the individual lashing out at me is going through a divorce, a tough time financially, a sickness, or perhaps they're just having a bad day?"

That's when I pray, "Holy Spirit, please help me to be sensitive to what is taking place."

I'm not making excuses for why people offend us, but sometimes those who are hurting are unable to control their feelings—and they hurt others.

Stop for a moment, swallow your pride, and consider the fact that we don't always have to be right. If you live your whole life trying to prove you're always perfect and everybody else is wrong, you're living in a fools paradise. That's not realistic; in fact it is unhealthy.

When you're involved in a battle, even if you feel justified, don't be obstinate and feel you must always come out on top. It's good to concede once in a while. Give people grace and cut them some slack.

Never allow someone else to interfere with your relationship with the Lord. There's a reason why people act the way they do. Ask the Holy Spirit to help you to be sensitive to the situation. Forgive them, let the problem go and, with God's help, move on.

Rule #8: Be Free

"Get rid of all bitterness, rage and anger, brawling and slander, along with every form of malice" (verse 31).

Do you know what happens if you put too much air pressure into an inner tube? Eventually it explodes!

When you deal with conflict the right way, the Lord will show you how to release the pressure valves of hostility, antagonism, temper, and so much more.

Remember, *"If the Son sets you free, you will be free indeed"* (John 8:36).

Rule #9: Be Kind, Compassionate, and Forgiving

"Be kind and compassionate to one another, forgiving each other, just as in Christ God forgave you" (verse 32).

Let's face it. People are not attracted to those who are volatile and angry. Yet, there are some Christian men and women who say, "I can't help it. That's just the way I am."

Well, it may be time for a turn-around. I probably don't have to remind you that the Bible declares, *"If anyone is in Christ, the new creation has come: the old has gone, the new is here!"* (2 Corinthians 5:17).

Since God has given you the freedom to choose:

- Why be angry when you can choose to be compassionate?
- Why be harsh when you can choose to be kind?
- Why hold grudges when you can choose to forgive?"

When you are constantly harboring resentment, you're the one who is enslaved. Ask the Lord to deliver you from an unforgiving spirit and to enlarge your compassion for your fellow man.

Since God has forgiven you, He is asking you to do the same.

Rule #10: Be Imitators of God

"*Therefore be imitators of God as dear children. And walk in love, as Christ also has loved us and given Himself for us, an offering and a sacrifice to God for a sweet-smelling aroma*" (Ephesians 5:1-2).

By using the word "therefore," Paul is letting us know, "I've written all these things to say this—be like the Lord!"

When a friend confronts you or your spouse is complaining, there's a sure-fire way to change the atmosphere. Take a deep breath, and ask yourself, "If Jesus were here, how would He respond in this situation?"

Well, the Lord is *always* with you! He is both our model and motivation. So instead of trying to solve the problem on your own, respond as Christ would. Be an imitator of Him.

I am praying that in every conflict—whether big or small—you will put these "Ten Rules of Engagement" into practice.

11
WISDOM FOR A GOOD NAME

A good name is more desirable
than great riches; to be esteemed
is better than silver or gold.
— PROVERBS 22:1

I own a Toyota with over 200,000 miles racked up on the odometer, so I have to take it to a service station every once in awhile to get an oil change and front end alignment. It's preventive medicine, you might say, because I've learned from experience that something that old can quickly break down. No matter how many years we have lived, it's easy to get off kilter.

In life, if we fail to stay on the straight and narrow road, our reputation can soon be shaky, even completely fall apart.

Should someone ask, "If you had to list two or three people who really have an exemplary name, who would they be?" You probably wouldn't have to think too long!

Now flip the coin and name some individuals who have a shoddy reputation. Again, certain people would spring to mind.

Personally I can think of men and women I've come in contact with who have plenty of influence, but the very mention of their name can create wrinkled brows and frowns.

In our key verse, Solomon is trying to keep our footsteps on track by saying that a good name is more valuable than all the riches of this world.

I am blessed that my parents, Jim and Bobbie George, have stellar reputations. A lady stopped me recently and told me, "I've worked with your mom for over 30 years"—then she went on to add what an honorable, trustworthy, godly woman my mother was. In addition, people continually cross my path who let me know the high regard they hold for my father.

However, just because my parents have an honorable reputation doesn't mean that I automatically qualify. I have to wake up every morning and pray, "Lord, help me not to focus on earthly gain, but to live a life that honors You."

COMMENDABLE CHARACTERISTICS

Think how awesome it would be if others were able to say about you: "He (or she) is faultless, righteous, has a reverence for the Lord and steers clear of wickedness."

Well, in Bible times there was such an individual. In fact, an entire book was written detailing his life: Job. *"In the land of Uz there lived a man whose name was Job. This man was blameless and upright; he feared God and shunned evil"* (Job 1:1).

I admire those characteristics and pray they can be said about me.

If you are blessed to have an A#1 reputation, don't just be thankful, you must guard it carefully. To put it bluntly: it can take twenty years to establish a good name, and five minutes to ruin it!

Regardless of the reputation of your parents or grandparents, you are writing you own story. If it is not up to biblical standards, with God's help that can all change. It starts with an internal decision, and in less time than you ever imagined, people will begin to view you differently.

SIX EMPOWERING PRINCIPLES

The foundation stones for building character that

138

brings honor to both you and your Creator, are found in His Word. There is wisdom for each of us in these divine principles:

First: Good People with Good Names Follow the Good Shepherd

Are you just an island to yourself, randomly making self-gratifying choices and soldiering on, doing things your way?

Instead of being led by you own experience, intellect, or carnal flesh, turn to the One who has the power and ability to help you make the right decisions.

This very moment, Jesus is telling you, *"I am the good shepherd. The good shepherd lays down his life for the sheep"* (John 10:11).

Every day we are confronted with situations that can either build or tarnish our reputations. By following a Shepherd that is *Good*, we can't go wrong.

Who are you following?

Second: Good People with Good Names are Good on the Inside Because of Jesus

Spiritual transformation has nothing to do with religion—which tries to force good behavior on a person from the outside, hoping it makes its way into their heart. But the spirit of religion is just an outward façade. It is impossible to be truly good without first being changed in your heart, soul, and mind.

When Jesus touches you on the inside, it will be evident in your behavior—which is how your name and reputation is established.

Have you ever driven through a neighborhood and glanced inside a few open garage doors? Some are neat and tidy, but the majority are a complete and utter mess—with boxes piled high and junk all over the place. Bikes with no wheels, a rusty mower that has cut its last lawn, faded Christmas decorations that have lost their sparkle!

Sadly, there are people everywhere who store up useless "stuff." Then, when a stressful situation crops up in their lives, what pours out of them is the very thing they've been hoarding.

Jesus addressed this issue when He declared, *"The good man brings good things out of the good stored up in him, and the evil man brings evil things out of the evil stored up in him"* (Matthew 12:35).

To me, this is a valid reason all believers should faithfully be in Church on Sunday with their Bibles open, worshiping, and receiving from the Lord. In the process they are storing up reserve power for when it is needed during the week when they face the stress of work, study, or family.

Since you are special in God's sight, make sure your life reflects this:

> *But you are a chosen people, a royal priesthood, a holy nation, a people belonging to God, that you may declare the praises of him who called you out of darkness into his wonderful light.*
>
> *Once you were not a people, but now you are the people of God; once you had not received mercy, but now you have received mercy.*
>
> *Dear friends, I urge you, as aliens and strangers in the world, to abstain from sinful desires, which war against your soul.*
>
> *Live such good lives among the pagans that, though they accuse you of doing wrong, they may see your good deeds and glorify God on the day he visits us"* (1 Peter 2:9-12).

Peter, the Apostle is referring to you and me. We are chosen, royal, holy, changed on the inside, and belong to God. Amen!

Third: People with Good Names do Good Works so that God Receives the Glory

It is totally impossible to earn the grace and mercy

of the Almighty. But because you have been redeemed it is only natural that your actions and deeds reflect what He has given.

Why do we help the poor and minister to those in need? It's not to place a spotlight on ourselves, but to glorify our Creator. As Jesus said, *"In the same way, let your light shine before men, that they may see your good deeds and praise your Father in heaven"* (Matthew 5:16).

May I share with you a personal example? I can't adequately express the value of the "works" the Lord has placed on my heart to do for the community. God has opened up so many doors for me, not because I'm a preacher, but for what people see in the projects I have undertaken. Most care little about my theology; what captivates them is my passion for the poor and needy.

Please understand, I have never done these things to receive accolades, but men and women are drawn to those who are engaged and active in good works. I've heard it countless times, "This is what the church is supposed to be doing."

As a result of giving all the honor and glory to God, I have been blessed to lead many to the Christ who placed this compassion in my heart.

Fourth: Good People with Good Names Surround Themselves with Good Influences

At several points in this book, I have emphasized the importance of being in the company of men and women with integrity and moral character.

When it comes to making or breaking a good name, people do not always solely make their judgments based on your behavior, but also on the actions of those with whom you associate. For example, if your friends are doing drugs, breaking their marriage vows, or using foul language, your image is being tarnished too.

We know that one rotten apple can spoil the whole barrel, so it may be time to sever certain relationships and surround yourself with godly individuals.

Fifth: Good People with Good Names are Good Among Bad People

As Christians, we've heard it mentioned a thousand times that we are "in the world but not of the world."

This means that in your daily walk you will be rubbing shoulders with all kinds of personalities and characters. Since this is true, if you are known to be a believer, others will be scrutinizing you with a magnifying glass. So make it your goal to live up to your reputation: *"Live such good lives among the pagans that, though they accuse you of doing wrong, they may see your good deeds and glorify God on the day he visits us"* (1 Peter 2:12).

As Paul wrote to young Timothy, *"He must also have a good reputation with outsiders, so that he will not fall into disgrace and into the devil's trap"* (1 Timothy 3:7).

Sixth: Good People with Good Names are Peacemakers, Not Drama Creators

Many carry the stigma of a lousy name because they continually feed off conflict and strife.

While Jesus walked this earth, He only became angry with the "religious" people; to everyone else He was a peacemaker.

If you want to protect or improve your reputation, at home, at church, and at work, start creating a culture of peace rather than a climate of drama.

Here is a proven prescription:

"Love must be sincere. Hate what is evil; cling to what is good. Be devoted to one another in brotherly love. Honor one another above yourselves. Never be lacking in zeal, but keep your spiritual fervor, serving the Lord.

Be joyful in hope, patient in affliction,

faithful in prayer. Share with God's people who are in need. Practice hospitality. Bless those who persecute you; bless and do not curse.

Rejoice with those who rejoice; mourn with those who mourn. Live in harmony with one another. Do not be proud, but be willing to associate with people of low position. Do not be conceited. Do not repay anyone evil for evil. Be careful to do what is right in the eyes of everybody.

If it is possible, as far as it depends on you, live at peace with everyone" (Romans 12:18).

I pray you will put these six empowering principles into practice. When you do, you will understand the wisdom of Solomon's counsel that a good name is more desirable than great riches.

12

WISDOM FOR WINNING

*If your enemy is hungry, give him food
to eat; if he is thirsty, give him water to drink.
In doing this, you will heap burning coals on
his head, and the Lord will reward you.*

– PROVERBS 25:21-22

I play racquet ball with a friend on a regular basis and sometimes when we arrive at the court we are both filled with more than our share of life's frustrations. We've even joked, "One of these days we need to write the names of people we are mad at on those racket balls—and hit them as hard as we can, as often as we can!"

But that is not the biblical approach to dealing with our enemies.

I don't know how you personally respond to your adversaries:

- Some like to face them head on.
- Some prefer to run away and hide.
- Some try to get even.
- Some become overwhelmed emotionally.

BETRAYED BY A KISS

As Jesus learned, some of your closest friends, may be the ones who turn on you.

The Bible chronicles how *"one of the Twelve—the one called Judas Iscariot—went to the chief priests and asked, 'What are you willing to give me if I hand him over to you?' So they counted out for him thirty silver coins. From then on Judas watched for an opportunity to hand him over"* (Matthew 26:14-16).

Notice the word "opportunity" that Judas was looking for. It is not my intention to make you fearful or paranoid, but there will be those in the world— your neighbors, relatives, even believers—who have the traits of Judas. They're strategic, calculating, looking for that moment of weakness, when they can inflict the most damage.

If the act of betrayal happened to the Son of God, it can happen to any one of us.

The word, *Judas* means "to kiss and poke with a spear." We know from the biblical account that Judas actually identified Jesus to His accusers by kissing Him on the cheek. At the same time, however he was figuratively stabbing the Lord in the back.

Not only did Jesus have enemies, but so did Solomon's father, King David, who wrote more about this topic than any other person in the Bible. In the book of Psalms, you find David being pursued by Saul's armies, crying out so many times, "God, help me! My foes are pursuing me. Lord, I need your wisdom and strength."

If Jesus encountered enemies and King David, whom God called, *"a man after My own heart"* (Acts 13:22), had foes, then, as a follower of Christ, you are likely to have them too.

COALS OF KINDNESS

We often think that the only way to defeat the opposition is with manmade artillery, but Solomon offered an alternative when he wrote that if your enemy is hungry or thirsty, give them food and drink. In doing so, *"you will heap burning coals on his head, and the Lord will reward you"* (Proverbs 25:22).

The phrase about coals is fascinating.

In Old Testament times, if you had a coal fire roaring, the goal was to keep it burning hot so your house would be warm and you'd be all set to cook a meal. If your coals burnt out, you would have to balance a small metal container on your head and walk to your neighbors and friends, asking for a few hot embers. Carrying them back home, the heat from the container would warm your entire body.

So the concept of heaping hot coals on a person's head is actually a sign of kindness.

To be rewarded by your heavenly Father, instead of plotting to get even, start showing goodness and mercy.

Ten Truths About Enemies

Before you can enter the winners circle, there are certain things you need to know—especially about those who are your adversaries:

Truth #1: Everyone Has Them

My grandfather once told me, "If you want to accomplish nothing, say nothing, do nothing, be nothing."

In life, we're going to face men and women who are insecure, jealous, and out to try and bring us down.

What should be our attitude toward them? Jesus offered this advice: *"You have heard that it was said,*

'Love your neighbor and hate your enemy.' But I tell you: Love your enemies and pray for those who persecute you" (Matthew 5:43-44).

Since opposition is inevitable on our earthly journey, take a moment to pause and send up a prayer for anyone who is against you—whether it is a competitor on the athletic field, a man or woman who is scheming behind the scenes for your job, or a jealous next door neighbor.

Truth #2: Enemies Should Not Drive us Away from God, but _to_ Him

Far too often, when we are confronted by another person, we become focused on their harsh words or attitude, and it causes us to be distracted and unproductive in our work.

Enemies have a way of pulling us into their negative web, and we quickly forget what the Lord has instructed us to do.

I'm sure there have been times when you could have echoed the words of the psalmist: *"Be merciful to me, O God, for men hotly pursue me; all day long they press their attack. My slanderers pursue me all day long; many are attacking me in their pride. When I am afraid, I will trust in you"* (Psalm 56: 1-3).

My prayer is that your foes will not hijack you

from your faith. Instead, like David, may they drive you *toward* trust in God. David used the enemy's negative momentum to push him into the arms of the Almighty.

Truth #3: Enemies can be Useful in Helping us Become More Like Christ

Perhaps you have asked, "God, why am I going through this? Why are they treating me this way?" Or, Lord, why are they saying this about me?"

The reality is that your heavenly Father will often use opposition to produce Christ-like character in you. It's what God's Word teaches: *"In this you greatly rejoice, though now for a little while you may have had to suffer grief in all kinds of trials. These have come so that your faith—of greater worth than gold, which perishes even though refined by fire—may be proved genuine and may result in praise, glory and honor when Jesus Christ is revealed"* (1 Peter 1:6-7).

Truth #4: Enemies Don't Magically Disappear

I recently had a situation that had no connection to our church. I began to hear that an individual, who happened to be a politician, was making negative, snide remarks about me to a few donors of our community food and outreach program. On hearing about it for the first two or three times, I gave him the benefit of the doubt. But after six or seven reports, I finally thought, "This doesn't seem to be going away, so I need to heap some coals on this man's head!"

I made an appointment with the individual, taking with me a list of statements he supposedly had made. Then I sat down with him as calmly, and as Christ-like as possible, but my tone was extremely firm—so much so that the person was soon almost begging me to stop, because I was confronting him with his own statements. This continued for several minutes.

I am pleased to report that our relationship has been restored and mended because I didn't assume that the issue was going to magically disappear. Instead I spoke to him in love and in the spirit of Christ.

Scripture counsels, *"Consider it pure joy, my brothers, whenever you face trials of many kinds"* (James 1:2),

The key word is that we have to *"face"* our trials. They're not going to vanish into thin air.

Truth #5: Enemies Sometimes Become Larger the More You Leave Them Alone

When a man or woman comes to me, complaining, "I have a problem with (so and so)," my first response is, "Have you talked to them about it?"

So often, they reply, "Well, no. I'm talking to you."

That's when I let them know, "Matthew 18 clearly states that you need to go the person you feel has maligned you."

Specifically, *"If your brother sins against you, go and show him his fault, just between the two of you. If he listens to you, you have won your brother over. But if he will not listen, take one or two others along, so that 'every matter may be established by the testimony of two or three witnesses.' If he refuses to listen to them, tell it to the church; and if he refuses to listen even to the church, treat him as you would a pagan or a tax collector"* (Matthew 18: 15-17).

Please don't be deceived into thinking you can just wait it out and ignore the problem; be wise and follow the instructions of Christ.

Truth #6: Enemies are Empowered by Supernatural Enemies

In some cases, a person in your life will say and do mean or unkind things against you. Well, they may not be totally to blame for their behavior! Why? Because they may be empowered by supernatural forces and are unaware of the harm they are inflicting.

Scripture tells us, *"For our struggle is not against flesh and blood, but against the rulers, against the*

153

authorities, against the powers of this dark world and against the spiritual forces of evil in the heavenly realms" (Ephesians 6:12).

Satan is never idle. He is always at work, entering into hearts and minds, causing them to commit unthinkable acts.

Never forget that Jesus, when He was on the cross, cried out in His last prayer, *"Father, forgive them; they don't know what they are doing"* (Luke 23:34).

Truth #7: Enemies Should Motivate Us to Live Peacefully with All Men

Anytime is the right time to mend fences, but the Christmas season is perfect for wrapping up things for the year.

If you can think of one person you've been at odds with, this specific holiday presents a wonderful opportunity to make a conscious decision that you are going to make things right.

Perhaps we need to take a clue from the angels, who said at the birth of Christ, *"Glory to God in the highest, and on earth peace, goodwill toward men"* (Luke 2:14 NKJV).

You have no idea how much it would mean when you decide to pick up the phone, or send a personal note or email to an individual that you may have had a few sharp words with in the past.

Back in the late 1980s, when Tammi and I were youth pastors at a mega church with about 6,000 members, there was a woman in the congregation that seemed to be at cross-hairs with 5,999 of them! She was mad at just about everybody.

Talk about drama! Practically every day we would hear of more conflict.

One Sunday morning the pastor announced, "We are going to take communion, but before we do, I am asking you to pause for a moment and take the opportunity to make things right with someone. If there is a person here that you are upset with, now is the time to make it right. And we're not going to approach the communion table until those things are resolved."

As God is my witness, this woman happened to be sitting on the front row, and a line formed all the way to the back of the sanctuary. It took nearly 45 minutes before communion could begin because that individual had so many people who wanted to "make things right."

God was at work. It was amazing to see the conflict resolution taking place that morning and it is a scene I'll never forget.

Paul the Apostle wrote, *"If it is possible, as far as it*

depends on you, live at peace with everyone" (Romans 12:18).

Truth #8: Enemies Can be Helpful in Exposing Truth

Listen carefully to those who have done you wrong, because chances are that in what they say, there is an element of truth. Don't throw the baby out with the bath water!

If your friends, neighbors, people in the church and the community are all repeating the same thing, it may be accurate—even if some of it originates with your enemies.

This can be hard and painful to go through, causing you to wonder, "God, how can you use that person to expose truth to me?"

Let me encourage you to make this your prayer: *"Teach me your way, O Lord; lead me in a straight path because of my oppressors. Do not turn me over to the desire of my foes, for false witnesses rise up against me, breathing out violence"* (Psalm 27:11-12).

When you hear negative complaints or opinions, ask the Holy Spirit to help you discern what is right.

Truth #9: Enemies Provide Us the Opportunity to Focus on and Worship God

In my experience, the best cure for dealing with

the pain caused by others, is to center my thoughts on the Lord and begin praising and worshiping Him. I lift my voice, saying, "God, help me and give me strength. Uncover any area of my life and help me to be pure. Lord, I worship you, Almighty God."

When you try to deal with opposition in your own strength, you grow tired and fatigued. How much better to look up and say, *"I call to the Lord, who is worthy of praise, and I am saved from my enemies"* (Psalm 18:3).

Truth #10: Enemies Will Not Have Victory Over You

"To you, O Lord, I lift up my soul; in you I trust, O my God. Do not let me be put to shame, nor let my enemies triumph over me" (Psalm 25:1-2).

Who will win the battle? Will it be Satan, who targets your soul, or God who will fight on your behalf and guarantee your ultimate triumph?

The foes we face in this life are not going to have victory over us, because we know the source of our strength and the fact that *"we are more than conquerors through him who loved us"* (Romans 8:37).

With Solomon you can stand to your feet and confidently declare, *"Victory rests with the Lord"* (Proverbs 21:31).

EXPRESS YOUR GRATITUDE

As you travel this journey, it is my prayer that you will read and re-read the chapters of this book until God's knowledge and wisdom permeates your life.

Take a moment to express your gratitude in advance for all of His bountiful favor and blessings. Say:

- "Thank You Lord, for wisdom in my life."
- "Thank You Lord, for wisdom that guides and protects."
- "Thank You Lord, for wisdom in my relationships."
- "Thank You Lord, for wisdom in temptation."
- "Thank You Lord, for wisdom during life's storms."
- "Thank You Lord, for wisdom in choosing friends."
- "Thank You Lord, for wisdom in correction."
- "Thank You Lord, for wisdom concerning Your destiny for me."
- "Thank You Lord, for wisdom that produces a happy heart."
- "Thank You Lord, for wisdom in conflict."

- "Thank You Lord, for wisdom to have a good name."
- "Thank you Lord, for the wisdom to win."

You will never be alone, wandering off-course when you receive and respond to God's *GPS— Guiding Principles for Success.*

FOR ADDITIONAL RESOURCES,
OR TO SCHEDULE THE AUTHOR FOR
SPEAKING ENGAGEMENTS, CONTACT:

SCOTT GEORGE
130 GALAHAD LANE
MAITLAND, FL 32761

PHONE: 407-579-8515
EMAIL: jscottgeorge1@gmail.com

OTHER BOOKS BY SCOTT GEORGE

LIVING BEYOND ORDINARY: DISCOVERING
AUTHENTIC SIGNIFICANCE AND PURPOSE
www.livingbeyondordinary.org

DOING GOOD, GREAT: 11 SECRETS
TO LIVING BEYOND ORDINARY
www.doinggoodgreat.org